Creating Inviting Schools

Edited by John M. Novak,
Wendy Rocca,
and Ann-Marie DiBiase

Published by
Caddo Gap Press

Creating Inviting Schools
Edited by John Novak, Wendy Rocca, & Ann-Marie DiBiase

Published by
    Caddo Gap Press
    3145 Geary Boulevard, PMB 275
    San Francisco, California 94118, U.S.A.

In cooperation with the
    International Alliance for Invitational Education

Price - $29.95

ISBN 1-880192-49-7

Library of Congress Cataloging-in-Publication Data
Creating inviting schools / edited by John Novak.
    p. cm.
    ISBN 1-880192-49-7 (alk. paper)
    1. Teaching. 2. Teacher-student relationships. 3. Motivation in
education. I. Novak, John M. II. Title.

    LB1025.2.C66 2006
    371.2--dc22

                                        2006002122

Contents

Dedication

John Novak

Thank you to the many educators around the world who have helped create inviting schools. Thank you to Linda and Natalie Novak who have helped create our inviting shared life.

Wendy Rocca

To my husband Pat, and my children, Jesse, Matthew, and Kristen, who have been my source of inspiration and motivation to continually improve who I am.

Ann-Marie DiBiase

To my mother Angela, for her unremitting invitations to life and unwavering support, and to the enduring memory of my grandmother Adelina Ungaro, for her quiet confidence and strength.

Foreword

William Watson Purkey

When John Novak, Co-founder of Invitational Education, first introduced me to the concept of "A Theory of Practice," I accused him of double-think. How could something be both a theory and a practice? Impossible! As usual, I was wrong. *Creating Inviting Schools* is a perfect example of how a concept can be both good theory and good practice.

Creating Inviting Schools is needed now more than ever. Education is ripe for a revolution. As the portly Mr. Oliver Hardy used to say, "This is another fine mess you've got us in." Our educational mess consists of mandatory retention of schools, high stakes testing, ruthless competition, zero tolerance, disheartened teachers, and other "disinviting" factors that contribute to mean-spirited schools. Perhaps never before has there been such a need for renaissance of trust, respect, and optimism, within a foundation of intentionality.

This book of reading brings together the stories of professional leaders who successfully applied invitational theory to the challenges and practice of real-life schools. Their rich insights into ways of applying a defensible theory to everyday practice will be an inspiration for anyone who reads this excellent book.

Chapter 1

Introducing Inviting
Schools in Action

John M. Novak and Wendy Rocca

How do we create schools and institutions of higher education where people want to be, want to learn, and want to support? It is not easy, but it can be done. A key ingredient in creating such welcoming and learning supportive places is the possession of a dynamic theory of practice, a self-correcting way of thinking about that which is worth doing well. Such a theory of practice would need to pay systematic attention to the ways different and subtle message environments call forth or negate human potential. Such a theory of practice would need to pay attention to the dedication and commitments of educators who systematically and creatively employ this approach. Such a theory of practice exists. It is called invitational education. This book presents examples of the work of educators in different positions of authority in different parts of the world dedicated to using this approach. It shows their intentions, strategies, successes, joys, and obstacles overcome in creating, developing, and sustaining inviting schools.

Invitational education is a self-concept approach to teaching, learning, and democratic practice that offers a perspective for addressing, evaluating, and transforming the total school environment. It is a set of interlocking assumptions, concepts, strategies, insights, and commitments that enables an educator to develop a focused framework for taking sustained and creative action. This approach rests on the following five assumptions:

1. People are valuable, able, and responsible and should be treated accordingly.

2. Education is a cooperative, collaborative activity.

3. The process is the product in the making.

4. People possess untapped potential in all areas of human endeavor.

5. Human potential can be realized best by places, policies, processes, and programs specifically designed to invite development and by people who are personally and professionally inviting with themselves and others.

Recognizing that people are never neutral, invitational educators recognize that everything and everybody in and around schools either calls forth or shuns human potential.

Originating in the book *Inviting School Success* (Purkey, 1978), and continuing to be refined and extended in other books (Purkey & Novak, 1984; Wilson, 1986; Purkey & Schmidt, 1987; Purkey & Novak, 1988; Purkey & Stanley, 1991; Novak, 1992; Purkey & Novak, 1996; Purkey & Schmidt, 1996; Purkey, 2000; Novak & Purkey, 2001; Novak, 2002; Purkey & Strahan, 2002; Purkey & Siegel, 2003), and carefully studied in dissertations (Inglis, 1976; Reed, 1981; Stehle, 1981; Amos, 1985; Radd, 1988; Chance, 1992; Asbil, 1994; Thompson, 2005) and philosophical papers, journal articles, and book chapters (Novak, 1978, 1984, 1985, 1986, 1999, 2003, 2005; McLaren, 1986; Pajares, 1994), the coming together of like minds and kindred spirits has culminated into an International Alliance for Invitational Education with more than 700 members throughout the world.

Invitational education is an evolving process that focuses on intentional actions. It is not something that happens by chance, it requires effort, dedication, and imaginative acts of hope. Participating in inviting schools can be joyous, humorous, exhilarating, and exhausting.

This book consists of thirteen stories told by educators who were able to establish and sustain a solid foundation of inviting practices. The joy, humor, exhilaration, and exhaustion of each story provides insights and strategies for all who wish to make their schools "the most inviting place in town." Here is an overview of each of the stories.

The Most Inviting Place in Town

"If it is to be, it is up to me" was the mantra of Kate Asbill, a double Inviting Award winning principal. Beginning by modeling the inviting message herself and decorating her office in magnificent style, she shows the steps to take in building an inclusive vision. She accentuates a variety of inviting practices with students, staff, and parents. Her enthusiasm is infectious.

The Calcium Primary School Story

Wendy Rocca tells the story how Harvey Smith, a university professor, and Lana Taylor, an elementary school principal, worked together to develop an award-winning showcase school. Located near a military base, the teachers and staff provide a needed family atmosphere for their students and parents who are far away from home and facing a world of diversity and change.

Inviting News from St. John Neumann School

With hard work, continual care, and a newsletter that celebrates success, St. John Neumann School increased its enrollment more than six-fold in 14 years. Barbara Cole, principal of this award winning schools shares the school's history, Pledge of Honor, and newsletter. Keeping everyone informed, involved, and invited is essential to create growth and retain a spirit of community.

Caring, Communication, and Collaboration:
A Professional Development Perspective

Sue Bowen, a superintendent of instruction and professional development coordinator, shows how to get things done from outside the school. Sharing her experiences in West Virginia and Kentucky, she outlines an 8-Step Method for developing a shared vision and connecting with other schools in the system. Thinking system-wide makes even better things happen as people grow through sharing and exploring.

Collaboration Through Commitment:
The Garfield Heights Story

The importance of collaboration in creating and sustaining inviting schools cannot be overemphasized. In this chapter, Judy Lehr, a consultant and university professor, worked with Superintendent Ronald Victor to develop system-wide implementation of the principles of invitational education. The needs of the heart are successfully connected to the development of facilities and academic goals.

Getting There:
Creating Inviting Climates

The inviting perspective is based on the perceptual tradition and self-concept theory. Tommie Radd builds on these interlocking foundations to develop a clear, concise, intentional plan for a positive guidance system and counseling program. The personal, emotional, behavioral, and social skills needed in life are learned in classroom "life labs" where individuality, connectedness, and development of potential are stressed.

A Guide to Inviting On-Line Education

Creating people-oriented schools in an era where many technological myths are being perpetuated is a challenging task for educators committed to an inviting perspective. Tony DiPetta, John Novak, and Zopito Marini present some prudent practical suggestions for using information and communication technology in elementary and secondary schools. In addition, they offer a checklist for discussion and reflection.

Inviting Parent Participation on School Councils

For many educators, parent involvement in schools can be either the best of times or the worst of times. In this chapter, Alice Schutz, Mary-Louise Vanderlee, and Rahul Kumar show what is involved in encouraging effective and authentic parental participation on school councils. Stressing the need for developing a well-established process for deliberation, the authors show what is involved in overcoming misunderstanding.

Creative Primary School:
From Passion to Action

This is the story of how an elementary school in Hong Kong embarked on the road to Invitational education. Beginning by attending a session on professional training, and then going to a conference and making connections with schools on another continent, Clio Chan and the teachers and staff of Creative Primary School have established an award-winning school that is visited by educators from around the globe.

Building the School as a Caring
and Collaborative Community

Hong Kong is a world-class city that is going through strenuous educational reforms. Priscilla Lee and Wendy Ho describe how Homantin Government Secondary School used and inviting framework to create an award-winning school. Showing examples of how people, places, programs, policies, and processes can come together in creative and sustaining ways, they provide inviting samples that can be used throughout the world.

Becoming Intentionally Inviting: A Case Study in Independent South African Schools

Many schools are already doing many inviting things that they just do not think about. In this examination of two schools, Nicky Aylmer, Di Dawes, and Martyn van der Merwe look at what is involved to taking the important step in becoming intentionally inviting. Knowing what you are doing and why you are doing it calls attention to all that is done in the school and makes transparent issues of control and openness.

Creating Schools That Invite Wellness

South Africa is a country with a history of racism, social strife, and economic tribulations. For an inviting approach to work here, it has to be well thought-out and sensitive to the present complexities. Linda Theron and Martyn van der Merwe show how the concept of wellness can be linked to the core principles of invitational education to provide a systematic and positive approach to school change.

Reaffirmation of Re-Accreditation through Invitational Education

For an idea to come alive it must first be born in our minds and then in our actions. Deborah Lonon shows how the inviting perspective came alive in the minds and practices of the faculty and staff at Ashville-Buncombe Technical Community College. Using the tenets of invitational education as their guide for their Quality Enhancement Plan, they created long-lasting changes and have become a beacon institution of higher education.

References

Asbill, K. N. (1994). Invitational leadership. Teacher perceptions of inviting principal practices. Doctoral Dissertation. New Mexico State University.

Chance, D. C. (1992). A study of five diverse middle schools and their efforts to bring about positive changes with at-risk students through invitational education. Doctoral Dissertation. The University of North Carolina at Greensboro.

McLaren, P. (1986). Interrogating the conceptual roots of invitational education—A review of Purkey and Novak's *Inviting school success*. *Interchange*, 17, 90-95.

Novak, J. M. (1978). Invitations to what? Paper presented at the American Educational Research Association Annual Conference, Toronto, Ontario, Canada.

Novak, J. M. (1984). Inviting research: Paradigm and projects for a theory of educational practice. Paper presented at the American Educational Research Association Annual Conference, New Orleans.

Novak, J. M. (1985). Invitational teaching for mere mortals. Paper presented at the American Educational Research Association Annual Conference, Chicago.

Novak, J. M. (1986). New directions with invitational education: Moving with McLaren from interrogation to conversation. *Interchange*, 17, 96-99.

Novak, J. M. (Ed.). (1992). *Advancing invitational thinking*. San Francisco: Caddo Gap Press.

Novak, J. M. (1999). Inviting criteria for democracy's schools. *Thresholds in Education, 25*(1), 4-6.

Novak, J. M. (2002). *Inviting educational leadership: Fulfilling potential and applying an ethical perspective to the educational process.* London, UK: Pearson.

Novak, J. M. (2003). Invitational leadership and the pursuit of educational living. In B. Davies & J. West-Burnham (eds.), *Handbook of educational leadership and management* (pp. 67-74). London, UK: Pearson.

Novak, J. M. (2005), Invitational leadership. In B. Davies (Ed.), *The essentials of school leadership* (pp. 44-60). London/New York: Sage.

Novak, J. M. & Purkey, W. W. (2001). *Invitational education.* Fastback 488. Bloomington, IN: Phi Delta Kappa Educational Foundation.

Pajares, F. (1994). Inviting self-efficacy: The role of invitations in the development of confidence and competence in writing. *Journal of*

Invitational Theory and Practice, 3, 13-24.

Purkey, W. W. (1978). *Inviting school success: A self-concept approach to teaching and learning.* Belmont, CA: Wadsworth.

Purkey, W. W. (2000). *What students say to themselves: Internal dialogue and school success.* Thousand Oaks, CA: Corwin Press.

Purkey, W. W. & Novak, J. M. (1984). *Inviting schools success: A self-concept approach to teaching and learning* (Second Edition). Belmont, CA: Wadsworth.

Purkey, W. W. & Novak, J. M. (1988). *Education: By invitation only.* Fastback #268. Bloomington, IN: Phi Delta Kappa.

Purkey, W. W. & Novak, J. M. (1996). *Inviting school success: A self-concept approach to teaching, learning, and democratic practice* (Third Edition). Belmont, CA: Wadsworth.

Purkey, W. W. & Schmidt, J. J. (1987). *The inviting relationship: An expanded perspective for professional counseling.* Englewood Cliffs, NJ: Prentice-Hall.

Purkey, W. W. & Schmidt, J. J. (1996). *Invitational counseling: A self-concept approach to professional practice.* Monterey, CA: Brooks-Cole.

Purkey, W. W. & Siegel, B. L. (2003). *Becoming an invitational leader: A new approach to professional and personal success.* Atlanta: Humanitics.

Purkey, W. W. & Stanley, P. H. (1991). *Invitational teaching, learning and living.* Washington, DC: National Education Association Library.

Purkey, W. W. & Strahan, D. B. (2002). *Inviting positive classroom discipline.* Westerville, OH: National Middle Schools Association.

Radd, T. R. (1998). The effects of grow with guidance on self-concept as learner and teacher self-concept. Doctoral Dissertation. The University of Akron.

Radd, T. R. (2000). Integrating self-concept into life skills. In C. L. Thompson & L. Rudolph, *Counseling children* (Fifth Edition) (pp. 152-155). Belmont, CA: Brooks/Cole.

Reed, C. (1981). Teacher invitations and effectiveness as reported by secondary students in Virginia. Doctoral Dissertation. The University of Virginia.

Stehle, C. F. (1981). Invitational learning. A case study on the implementation of the sustained silent reading (SSR) program within the junior high school classroom. Doctoral Dissertation. The University of Rochester.

Thompson, D.R. (2005). Invitational education within an ethic of care: Creating an inviting school culture. Doctoral Dissertation. Stephen F. Austin State University.

Wilson, J. H. (1986). *The invitational elementary classroom.* Springfield, IL: Charles C. Thomas.

Chapter 2

"The Most Inviting Place in Town"

Kate Asbill

Inviting schools do not happen by accident. Inviting schools are carefully constructed, one day at a time. Every action, every interaction, every reaction, every inaction adds together to create the whole. Every person, every part of the place, every policy, every program, every process, matters. Everything counts. Everything adds to or takes away from the whole. Each idea that surfaces for consideration, each dream that is envisioned, each moment matters.

My name is Kate Asbill. I was the principal of two schools where invitational education was intentionally practiced. Both schools, Grand Heights Early Childhood Center in Artesia, New Mexico, and Holloman Primary School on Holloman Air Force Base near Alamogordo, New Mexico, received the Inviting School Award. Each time, this honor was achieved after many people worked toward that shared vision for more than five years. Since that time, I have worked as an invitational education consultant and have assisted six other schools in earning that distinction. In this chapter, I will share experiences, insights, and inspiration to assist others in their quest to create an Inviting School.

Start Somewhere

One might ask, "Where do we start? Where do we begin in the creation of an inviting school?" We must "START SOMEWHERE." We must take that first step and invite others to follow. If we have a dream of how a school should or could be, we must share it. If we have an idea, a vision, it is our responsibility to help others see the possibilities. We need to enroll others in that vision. Before leaders can help others to have clarity of purpose—a clear concept of what it is that is to be accomplished and why—the mission must first be personalized.

As a person who wanted to lead others toward a positive dream, I thought, "If it is to be, it must begin with ME." This quotation by Epictetus was my mantra: "Say to yourself what you would be; then do what you have to do."

Armed only with a desire in my heart to do something different, to do something special, to do something right, I knew that I must first dare to do. I believe that when we do, others will too. Others will resonate in reaction when they see our example. If it is your desire to create a more inviting school, this is my best advice: As you examine each area of your school and search for the place to begin, I think you will find that the best place to start is in your own heart.

As a principal with a desire to create a place that deserved distinction as an Inviting School, it was necessary to begin with myself. Knowing I could control only my own actions, I knew I must first model the message. In order to help others see clearly the concepts of invitational education (IE), I had to make invitational education come to life. I had to paint a picture of how things could be, and it had to begin with me. My behavior toward others had to be mentally monitored and the formation of trusting relationships had to be a priority.

The next step was to start with my space, my place - the principal's office. Often people have a preconceived idea of how that place will look and what is to happen there. The initial changes caught the attention of those that passed or entered. It was a tiny office; but as I added color and carefully created a cozy haven, it came to life and soon they saw a visible difference. Where there was somber sameness, dreary green hospital-like walls and cold, barren floors, I added a cheerful collection of carefully chosen items. I observed individuals as they walked by, stopped and craned their necks to peek inside. "It's working," I thought. "I have their attention," I told myself.

The children were the first to comment. Amber was sent to the office for something—something naughty she had done, I'm sure. She walked in and sullenly said, "This looks like a kid's room." I don't think she meant it as a compliment; but to me it was. "Thank you, it is," I said, " I really want you and the other children to come to the office when you're not in trouble, when you have something to share, and when you need someone to talk to." It was Amber who helped me realize that kids who cause problems have problems. I was able to help her as our relationship evolved, but it all started with her astute observation that my office looked like a kid's room.

Another day, another little girl came in. After looking around carefully, she said, "You must really like...kids." I had expected her to say teddy bears or beavers since she could see them everywhere she looked, but she saw beyond the bears and beavers. My heart sang when she repeated, "You must really like kids." I said, smiling, "I do." She added, "You must like them a lot." "I do." "My mama doesn't like kids. Well, she likes them, she just doesn't like to be around them." "Oh," was all I could say before she added, "She works at day care. They have twelve little rug rats over there."

It was working. If the children could see it, I knew the adults would get the message sooner or later. So, I continued to unveil the vision by creating an inviting atmosphere in the outer office.

Warm Welcome

The first person people meet upon entry into a school is the secretary; therefore, she must understand her important role. I knew invitational education was a theory of practice, and the place it had to be practiced was the principal's office. It had to start from the first phone call or entrance into the building. Getting the secretary to see the importance of intentionally treating each person with respect is paramount to the process. Each person who enters must be treated with dignity and respect and given a warm welcome that sends this message: "We're so glad you're here!"

On my third day as principal of the primary school at Holloman Air Force Base, one helpful teacher took it upon herself to teach me about rank. She came with a list with lines and designs and carefully explained to me how to distinguish the "privates from the powerful." I listened politely, took her list and placed it in a desk drawer. Six years later when I left, I laughed when I found that list where I had tucked it away that third day. I meant no disrespect when I formulated my plan to never learn about rank, to never know whose parents should be held in higher regard than others. It seemed to me—children didn't have rank. It became my policy in the principal's office to treat everyone as if they were the general's kids (or was that the commander's kids?). I never could remember what to call the guy in charge. I did call him, "Sir"; but everyone got the same royal treatment.

Supportive Stay

After the warm greeting, the next step was to insure a supportive stay. I began to "preach" the philosophy of "inviting school success":

◆ Students must experience success every day. If they are not learning the way we are teaching, then we must teach the way they learn.

◆ Treat everyone with trust and respect. They will respond in a like manner.

◆ Teaching isn't telling. Teach students, not subjects.

◆ All students can learn. They may not all learn on the same day or in the same way, but all children can learn.

◆ Find out where students are and take them as far as you can in that school year. If they are in your room, their learning is your responsibility.

◆ Self-concept and school achievement go hand and hand. How students perceive themselves will determine what they will attempt to achieve.

◆ Don't ask, "Is this kid smart?", but rather, "How is this kid smart?"

◆ Teach the children, "It's not that you can't do it, you just haven't done it yet."

◆ Celebrate learning. Each attempt is a victory.

◆ Keep kids as excited about school and about learning as they are when we get them in kindergarten. Learning can be fun.

◆ Educators need to make every effort to keep themselves as excited about teaching as when they started their career or a new school year.

◆ Educators are not to be dispensers of discipline, but rather teachers of social skills.

◆ Our school can be "the most inviting place in town."

Fond Farewell

In addition to the need for a warm welcome and a supportive stay, we found there was also a need for a fond farewell. Because of the mobile nature of our military families, we were sensitive to the needs of those who were leaving and those who were left behind. Just as we gave special attention to each student as they arrived, we were careful to give positive, supportive attention as they left us. It was our goal for the students and their parents to always look back on their stay in our school as a memorable and meaningful time in their lives.

We often spoke of those who had left us in order to let the children know that they would not be forgotten when it was their turn to leave our school. We encouraged the children to stay in touch through the exchange of addresses and phone numbers. Making lasting connections with classmates and staff members can strengthen the loyalty felt toward an institution and foster fond remembrance of their time in your school. While providing a warm welcome, a supportive stay and a fond farewell will do much toward promoting positive perceptions of a school, it is essential to emphasize that schools are for learning, and the primary purpose of that institution is to provide inviting instruction.

Inviting Instruction

Always remember that the ultimate purpose for creating an inviting school is to create an optimal learning environment. The most inviting thing you can do for your students is teach them the skills and attitudes they need to be successful. The book *Inviting School Success* (Purkey & Novak, 1996) offers a blueprint for building a community where teachers want to teach and children want to learn. The people, places, policies, programs, and processes all work together to invite the potential of all who enter. It is our desire to create centers for learning that help children to find the talents and abilities they possess and to spark in them an awareness of their unique place in this world. Presenting the things that are to be learned in an inviting manner is the charge and challenge of each educator. Provide age-appropriate instruction, information and activities.

◆ Plan daily for a variety of learning strategies to address different learning modalities.

◆ See that supplies and support are available, equipment is in good repair, and that the building is properly maintained. Other school personnel can take care of these responsibilities in order to allow teachers uninterrupted time to teach the children.

◆ Guard instruction time jealously. Do everything in your power to prevent the "fragmented day" that steals momentum and interrupts the learning process. Keep teaching time sacred.

◆ Adopt the philosophy that it is better to ask for forgiveness than permission. Trust the teachers to do what they do best—teach.

◆ Form teams of teachers to work together toward improving individual student achievement and understanding.

◆ Encourage and expect experimentation and discovery.

◆ Celebrate the learning that will take place in such an environment.

Teachers can remain enthusiastic the entire year and throughout their educational careers when their ideas are valued and they are encouraged and allowed to be life-long learners. When teachers work collegially on meaningful school projects that benefit the staff and students, relationships are formed, loyalties are strengthened, and feelings of ownership evolve. It is a basic human need to be part of a cause beyond oneself. Lives are enriched and more meaningful if teachers believe they are called to the cause of providing an optimal learning environment, complete with instruction that invites growth. When a safe haven where students and staff learn together is created, all who enter will be blessed by their association with the institution.

Having a Safe Haven

As I write this chapter, a war on terrorism is being waged and the need for creating a safe haven for children is highlighted. In an age of violence, fear, and anger, it is more imperative than ever that we make our schools and classrooms kinder, gentler places. Encourage all staff to work together as a team to form a functional family feeling in the entire school. Put processes into place that send these messages to students, staff, and parents: "Welcome home." "It is safe here." "We care about you and we are glad you are here."

Theory into Practitioners

While trying not to overuse the "I" (inviting) word, I looked for ways to introduce this powerful theory of practice known as invitational education. Every day in a variety of ways, it was my goal to put that "theory into practitioners." As Purkey and Novak, (1996) state, with any idea there are four stages of implementation: awareness, understanding, application, and adoption. These sequential stages take place over a period of months and years. Invitational education is a slow-growth process—a transformational process that takes time. It does not happen overnight or without conscious, intentional effort.

As the staff began to gain an awareness of invitational education, there were those who were quickly attracted to the idea. Some seemed to reach the next stage of understanding sooner than others. While continuing to invite everyone, more energy was expended toward working with those who were eager to learn about the philosophy. Those individuals who were already functioning at the unintentionally inviting level of relating were the first to grasp the concept, and they wanted to know and do more. It was interesting to watch their initial attempts at the application of inviting behaviors.

Since any attempt is a victory, we built on our successes and learned from our mistakes. Moving to the final stage of idea implementation requires time and constant monitoring.

The concept of creating an inviting school is contagious. Speak of the vision and paint a picture of how things can be. Work with those who nod and smile and keep encouraging others to enroll. At each faculty meeting take time to tell of things that are being done to make your school the most inviting place in town. Specific things that can be done to introduce a staff to IE are:

◆ Join the Alliance for Invitational Education. Institutional memberships are available.

◆ Visit the IE website at www.invitationaleducation.net for information and ideas.

◆ Show the *Video Journal of Education on Invitational Education (Vol. 2 No. 1)*.

◆ As professional developmental plans are decided upon, encourage staff members to write plans that allow learning more about the philosophy.

◆ Purchase several copies of *Inviting School Success* (Purkey & Novak, 1996) and have key people begin reading and discussing it. Use a book club format to stimulate conversation.

◆ Purchase PDK Fastback #488 (2001) (*Invitational Education*) for each member of the staff.

◆ Use brainstorming techniques to involve all in the process.

◆ Implement ideas generated by those who show interest.

◆ Address concerns of those who are curious or cautious.

◆ Encourage each staff member to make an intentional effort to take care of themselves and their colleagues. Remember, "No one can teach on an empty spirit."

◆ Model for them the importance of nurturing, caring relationships.

◆ Make a sign that says: "The quality of adult relationships within a school has more to do with the quality and character of the school and with the accomplishments of students than any other factor." (Barth, 1990)

Remember the Alliance adages, "Process is as important as product" and "Process is product in the making." Each step along the way toward the goal is to be savored and enjoyed. In actuality, one can never say, "We have arrived"; therefore, it is important to celebrate every victory and build upon each success. When I visualize the inviting process, I see it as an upward spiral, described as a helix by Purkey and Novak (1996), in Chapter 8 of *Inviting School Success*.

Becoming an Inviting School

It has been my observation that if a group of leaders in a school set a goal of achieving the Inviting School Award, an honor bestowed by the Alliance for Invitational Education on schools that intentionally exemplify the philosophy; it will help to keep the focus on the vision. Someone must assume the responsibility of coordinating efforts and maintaining focus on the desired goal.

It is realistic to set a timeline of three to five years for the culmination of those efforts. Some schools have attained this award in a shorter period of time; but because of my belief that "process is as important as product," I encourage people to set their goals and begin taking baby steps in that direction. In my estimation, those schools that consciously work together toward being deserving of the distinction as an Inviting School are more likely to create a truly inviting environment. Intentionality is the key to becoming an Inviting School and also to sustaining the invitational spirit once the award has been received.

Consciously Creating Inviting Schools

To move a group of educators from the awareness and understanding levels to those of application and adoption, following are additional ideas I have gleaned from my experience. In my observation, the best way to get the entire staff on board for the journey toward becoming an inviting school is to have a retreat dedicated to the comprehension of the philosophy of invitational education. When a group gathers away from the usual work site in comfortable surroundings, much can be accomplished. Because relationships are an integral part of the invitational process, the retreat setting is ideal for learning about the concept. When colleagues come together with time for laughing, learning, and eating, something magical happens; and bonds are built that will strengthen the school.

◆ Barth (1990) points out that the nature of adult relationships within a school is vital for school quality, character, and achievement. Time spent cultivating closeness and caring among the adults in the school will be beneficial to all who work and study there.

◆ It is also effective to have traditional in-service provided by long marchers from the Alliance for Invitational Education. Educators can move more quickly from awareness to adoption when exposed to a variety of viewpoints concerning this theory of practice. Invite practitioners who have experienced success with creating inviting atmospheres and expose your staff to those mentors. A list of experienced presenters is available through the Alliance Speaker's Bureau.

◆ Arrange site visits for key people from your building. Allow the leaders from your school to travel to other Inviting Schools so they can experience first hand how it feels to enter a place that has been designated "the most inviting place in town."

◆ Find ways to fund your staff to attend the annual meeting of the Alliance for Invitational Education. Host gatherings in your area and invite leaders from the Alliance to attend and participate in the program. Share the vision with others in your district and state. As the teachers gain confidence and knowledge, encourage them to share what has been done in your school and help other interested educators hear the message of how an optimal learning environment can be created through the intentional use of IE practices.

◆ Guide the group in your charge to adopt as their goal to become a school that deserves the Inviting School Award. Make it known that your school will not be nominated until everyone in the school becomes intentional about exemplifying the stance of invitational theory. Help your staff to understand that everyone and everything adds to or takes away from the whole.

◆ Encourage each individual to do his or her part in the process. It only takes one negative interaction to undo much good that has been accomplished. Establish the language of invitational education as the official language of your building. This language of transformation can be used to help hasten the process from awareness to adoption. For example, when everyone on the staff knows about "blue cards" and " orange cards," negative and positive interactions are readily identified. IE terminology can guide your staff members toward their goal.

◆ Realize and reiterate that no one is perfect. When someone slips into a lower level of behavior and behaves in a disinviting manner - and they will- just encourage them to learn the lesson and try hard to get back on track.

As a conscious, concerted and sustained effort is made to educate everyone in the building about invitational education, positive systemic change will occur. A transformation will take place in the people and the place and the ultimate result will be student success. To be most effective, the entire staff will be intentionally exposed to and encouraged to adopt the ideals of invitational philosophy. As with any new idea, those involved will move from awareness to understanding, to application, and then to adoption of the theory of practice. Remember to think of it as putting "theory into practitioners."

As stated earlier, this does not happen by accident, but it can happen through the careful orchestration of invitations to enroll in the vision of creating an Inviting School. After that decision has been made, begin taking the necessary steps to see that it happens. Although achievement of the Inviting School Award does not mean a school has "arrived," it is a meaningful honor and marks a significant milestone in the life of the institution.

Inviting Involvement

It has been my experience that utilizing the assistance of volunteers can greatly enhance all that happens in a school setting. Invite volunteer involvement. Research has shown that the number one complaint parents have about schools is that they do not feel welcome. For this reason, actively inviting parents to participate is strongly recommended.

At both Grand Heights and Holloman Primary, we welcomed parents and other volunteers to assist us in many ways. Lessons were learned and I will share some of them with you. The best "PR" (public relations) program that you can have for your school is a well-coordinated volunteer program. As people work in your building on a day to day basis, they will see the exciting things that are going on and they will tell others what they have observed. They will find that it is a safe, welcoming place for them and for their children. They will become a part of the school family.

At Holloman Primary, Sheryl Sunada was our parent volunteer coordinator. Having an enthusiastic committed person in that position was most beneficial. One school year we had more than 10,000 hours of recorded volunteer help. Much was accomplished. Following are suggestions of things we learned about inviting volunteer involvement:

Volunteers

◆ Invite them.
◆ Instruct them.
◆ Respect them.
◆ Involve them.
◆ Appreciate them.

Invite Them

There are people who would like to help in your school. Make parents and others feel welcome there.

◆ Send an invitation—let people know that you welcome them in your school and that you could use their help. Ask them to be your partners.

◆ Get the message across through your parent organization, parent meetings, newsletters, and through your words and actions—PARENTS ARE NEEDED IN THIS SCHOOL!

◆ Have a volunteer form and ask people to sign up. Make a list of these names. If they turn the form in, assume they mean it and make a conscientious effort to call each person during the year.

◆ Offer several levels of involvement. List areas of need (district level, school level, class level).

Instruct Them

◆ Hold a workshop for volunteers involved at the classroom instructional level.

◆ Request a commitment of regular help.

◆ Explain the need for dependability. Teachers will be counting on them to meet the objectives for the day. Ask regular volunteers to call if they can't come.

◆ Ask helpers to arrive early to get instructions before the children are in the room.

◆ Discuss the importance of appearance—stress proper dress.

◆ Tell them that younger children are not to come along when the volunteer helps in the classroom.

Respect Them

◆ Let volunteers know that you look forward to their help.

◆ Encourage teachers to PLAN AHEAD. Plans should be in writing. Volunteers have to feel that their time is well spent.

◆ Give volunteers stimulating things to do.

◆ Capitalize on their strengths and interests.

◆ Suggest several ways that they might be helpful and allow them to choose an activity with which they feel comfortable. Respect their preferences.

◆ Allow volunteers to start out slowly—working first on a one-to-one basis, then progressing to a small group.

◆ Talk to them about what they will be doing the next time they come.

◆ Let them take home materials that they will be using in order to familiarize themselves with the lesson.

Involve Them

Involve parents in the learning process even if they are unable to come to the school regularly. Consider these strategies:

◆ Offer meaningful parent programs such as "How to Help Your Child in School."

◆ Keep lines of communications open between home and school.

◆ Include parent/child activities in class or school newsletters.

◆ Send home job calendars that have daily suggestions for parent/child interactions.

◆ Send home notes to let parents know what you are working on at school. Ask for their help.

◆ Encourage parents to help with extra credit home projects to extend classroom learning.

◆ Make an effort to plan activities to continue parental involvement throughout the school year.

Appreciate Them

◆ Always make volunteers feel welcome and glad they came!

◆ Express gratitude—say "Thanks!"

◆ Recognize them in the school newsletter and arrange for an article in the local newspaper to tell about their activities.

◆ Invite them to eat in the cafeteria on special occasions.

◆ Take an interest in their personal lives. (Remember their birthdays and ask about their families).

◆ Present them with certificates or small remembrances to let them know that you don't take them for granted. Present these in front of the children.

◆ Send postcards of appreciation for participation.

◆ Send small notes that say "Thanks for sending the delicious snacks today!" It will take a minute and will be remembered much longer.

◆ Everyone has a desire for recognition. Nurture your volunteers with sincere appreciation. Keep a record of volunteer hours. Have them sign in and out. This record of volunteer time will make everyone even more aware of how parental involvement can help principals, teachers, and students.

Consider the potential of parent power! In times of budget cuts and negative school publicity, this often untapped resource is waiting to be discovered and invited forth!

Exemplifying Efforts

I have witnessed many examples of how intentional efforts at creating a more inviting school have had a positive effect on a school community. Let me share some of those success stories with you.

When I first arrived at Holloman Primary School, I walked into the auditorium and thought, "This is the ugliest room I've ever seen in my life."

No one knew it yet, but that room became a priority; and I began to formulate an idea for the Auditorium Transformation. As time went by, others were enrolled in the vision and something synergistic took place and the final results far exceeded any idea I had originally conceived.

Virginia Weaver, who had taught at that school for more than 20 years, had always wanted to improve the appearance of the meeting room; and this project gave her a chance to put her creative talents to work. She recruited other willing workers and they designed, painted, and perfected the southwestern style wall decorations. Countless hours were donated to creating a beautiful, inviting place to assemble. A local artist painted a lovely mural to complement the Southwest motif.

In my 12 years of being a principal, I only initiated one out-of-school fund-raiser; and it was to generate funds for the window shades and a stage curtain to complete the auditorium transformation. We told the children the purpose of the project; then I promised them if they would sell $6,000 worth of candy, I would kiss a pig. They really wanted me to kiss that pig, so many of the children and their parents joined the efforts to earn money to improve the appearance of the auditorium and to see that promise fulfilled. It is interesting to note that they sold $16,000 worth of candy.

Yes, I kissed the pig!

We found it funny that it was February, Dental Health Month, and the base dentist's wife, Paula Fuller, was our project chairperson. Everyone involved felt proud of the culmination of efforts. Many benefits beyond a beautiful room were gleaned from the transformation of the auditorium.

When Mrs. Weaver remembers her time at Holloman, one of her favorite memories is her many volunteer hours spent painting graphics on the walls. I will never forget the way she took a tiny brush and carefully re-painted each line to assure that it was straight. Friendships were formulated that will last forever during that and other school improvement projects.

Another example is the "labor of love weekend of work" that was given as a gift for our staff. District funds were secured for improving the appearance of the lounge, and parents were recruited to secretly redecorate the teacher's lounge as a surprise for the staff. The teachers left on Friday after school, parents arrived with pails of paint and worked until 10 each night throughout the weekend to create a lovely "recovery room" for the teachers and support personnel. I'll never forget the pleasure experienced by each person who walked in on Monday morning.

Those that did the work greeted teachers, and there was a cake that was decorated with the phrase, "We love you." The freshly painted walls were decorated with designs that matched the curtains, bulletin board backgrounds, and table decorations. Green plants were on the window-sills. New furniture and carpets complemented the decor. Each time they entered the lounge, people were reminded that they were loved and appreciated. Although these two examples describe the improvement of the "place," there were many benefits that eternally touched the people involved. The far-reaching effects of everyone's efforts will never be known.

My favorite of our improvement efforts was the Playground Beautification project at Holloman Primary School. Holloman Air Force Base is located in the desert southwest. When I arrived it was disappointing to see the desolate, barren playground without grass, one lone tree, and ancient playground equipment. As with the ugly auditorium, I immediately saw a need for improvement and envisioned a time when there would be not only grass and trees, but also shaded benches, drinking fountains and safe, modern playground equipment.

The kindergarten teachers and parents initiated the first efforts toward improvement. The $60.00 raised by that group was used to purchase five globe willow trees. A Saturday workday of donated labor made a difference. As time went by others joined the initiative and $1,600.00 was raised. A partnership was formed with the parent advisory council and the Holloman Civil Engineering Squadron. Landscaping plans were interrupted by the Iraqi invasion of Kuwait and hundreds of Holloman parents were sent to defend Saudi Arabia with Operation Desert Shield and Desert Storm.

After several months, most parents returned; and the "Desert Storm" playground project was continued with renewed enthusiasm. A $75,000 landscaping grant was written and received. The participative attitude among school personnel and volunteers generated the development of a three-school campus master plan.

Major Roger Sunada, landscape architect and project organizer, wrote this in his letter of nomination for Holloman Primary to receive the Inviting School Award: "Students were interviewed and involved. The youngest students drew pictures of playground equipment and features they wanted to see. Teachers, custodians, office staff, school board members, and parents were all involved in the planning. The $75,000.00 grant money was spent on materials for more asphalt for playgrounds, sprinkler systems, grass, parking lots, benches, new playground equipment, block retaining walls, trees and shrubs. Virtually all of the labor was donated. The total project would have cost more than $250,000.00 dollars if it had been contracted."

The efforts of many volunteers and staff members brought this vision into reality. One story we love to tell is about the night Sheryl Sunada was at the school watering the grass. At midnight, the Military Police came to the playground to see what she was doing. Thank goodness, she was not arrested! This type of dedication to the cause was something amazing that we saw from our volunteers.

Colonel Gordon Janiec and his wife, Cherie, were other volunteers who wholeheartedly participated in these projects. Colonel Janiec left Holloman and returned to the base at a later time with the intention of completing the master-plan and eventually encompassed the entire base in the beautification project. The Desert Storm Playground Beautification project was a huge success in many ways. The estimated monetary value was monumental—starting with the $60.00 seed money earned for the kindergarten project and leading to the grant and the successful implementation of the master plan.

As with the Auditorium Transformation Project, unknown benefits were derived from the involvement of students, parents, and staff in a creative project that has continued to bless school patrons for years since its completion. Lifelong friendships were formed, new talents were discovered, and precious memories were made. You can't put a price tag on those things.

As time goes by and memory dims the details, one might wonder, "Was it really that way? Did we actually create a school climate that could be called 'the Most Inviting Place in Town'? Was it really a special place for parents and students?" I have Roger's nomination letters and others that were written in support of the Inviting School nomination. A beautiful memory book was made by Mary Helen Mertz, a kindergarten teacher, and submitted to the Alliance which provides a lovely snapshot of what existed at that time. These things substantiate that success. Most of all, I have continuing relationships with friends who shared that memorable experience.

Sustaining the Spirit

As stated earlier, receiving the Inviting School Award does not mean that you "have arrived." After the honor has been achieved, it is even more essential to show through example what it means to be inviting; this will require a great deal of intentionality.

After a school has received the Inviting School Award, it is imperative to continue a concerted effort of sustaining the spirit of invitational education. As time passes and people come and go, those that remain must be thoroughly grounded in the philosophy and their belief that remaining an Inviting School is a priority. An on-going emphasis on the importance of maintaining an optimal learning environment through the monitoring of inviting practices is needed.

Hiring the Right People

The hiring, induction, and indoctrination of new people is the most important element in sustaining the spirit that has been established in an institution. The most effective way to assure continuity of purpose is to hire the right people as positions become open. The people in the process are the most important of the "5 Ps," and it is paramount that the right people are selected. This can be accomplished by a committee of concerned staff members or by a principal or personnel director who is attuned to attitudes and philosophies consistent with invitational theory.

When hiring persons for any position in the school, choose carefully. Janitors, teachers, assistants, cafeteria workers, counselors, secretaries, and principals will all come into contact with the children. Choose caring, conscientious individuals because they will impact many. Tell each applicant of your goal of creating an inviting educational environment and watch their reactions and listen to their words. As new staff members come on board, make an intentional effort to educate them about the philosophy and help them to feel like a valuable part of the group. Each new hire brings ideas and energy that can make or break the cycle of positive change that has been carefully created.

The need for INTENTIONALITY in the hiring process was highlighted to me recently. Purkey sent me a letter from a school that had received the Inviting School award several years ago. Apparently the school had received an invitation to the World Conference of the Alliance for Invitational Education. The new principal wrote back, "We are no longer an Inviting School. We now do Success for All, Purkey's note to me said, "Doesn't this bring a tear to your eye?" I wrote back, "Yes, it does and also an ache to my heart."

Invitational education is all about inviting school success and is consistent and compatible with the Success for All programs. One does not have to go away for the other to exist. Invitational education is not like the flavor of the month. It is not just another quick-fix or fad for schools to try and then abandon for another

29

method or passing fancy on the pendulum of change. After more than 30 years in education, and 50 in schools, I have seen many programs come and go. Invitational education is different. It is not something that will go out of style or get antiquated. IE is a timeless philosophy founded upon principles that are proven and will continue to be effective always. I know from personal experience that this philosophy is one that works as well today as it has through the years.

When the ideal level of "adoption" has been reached and sustained by a school staff, educators will be intentionally inviting both personally and professionally. Intentional invitational living will become a way of life that transforms classrooms, schools, people, and the world.

Intentional Invitational Living

In 1985, I attended my first invitational education conference in Greensboro, North Carolina. After I was there for a few days of meeting and interacting with members, I began to realize that what they were talking about was not just Invitational education. It was something bigger, something more, and something personal. What they were talking about and modeling was really intentional invitational living. As I observed the people and got to know them, I knew that they believed in the Invitational Philosophy and that they put the principles of the philosophy into practice in their everyday lives. They spoke of invitational education as being a theory of practice and I came to understand that it is not something that you turn on and off at the school house door. It is a way of life, a way of being, a way of relating to everyone you meet.

Years of close interaction and communication with those who espouse this philosophy has confirmed my initial feeling that the people who practice the invitational philosophy are consistent in their stance, and others notice their positive presence.

I see clearly that this philosophy of invitational education is really a philosophy of life. It is about the way we live our lives each day, both in and out of schools.

Invitational living is about relationships; it is about how people interact one with another. It is based on a foundation of caring. Invitational living is about attitude, consistency, and intentionality. Invitational living is about making a conscious daily decision to make a positive difference in our world.

Intentionality is what sets this philosophy apart. As stated earlier, Inviting Schools do not happen by accident. In order to create a culture of caring, a conscious choice has to be made by those who work in schools to intentionally conduct themselves in an inviting manner. As people become more conscious of their behavior and choose certain attitudes and actions, chances are that they will behave in better ways than when thoughtless action prevails. The invitational stance of trust, respect, optimism and intentionality gives guidance to our daily dealings with others. It is the stance we take when a decision must be made. It is the gauge for good choices in a myriad of options. This will lead to invitational learning and living.

Reflecting

As we consider what is necessary to create and sustain Inviting Schools, let us reflect upon lessons learned from my work with schools and school personnel. It takes at least one person who has a vision for that institution—one enthusiastic, energetic person who enrolls others in that vision. It takes an intentional effort to educate the entire staff about the philosophy and requires teaching everyone in the school the IE language of transformation and speaking that language to each other on a daily basis. It requires a continual monitoring of all aspects of the school—examining the 5 P's with systematic, sustained effort.

If the desired result is to create inviting classrooms, schools and homes, we first visualize how things can be; then do what needs to be done to reach that end. In order to make ideas come to pass, certain steps can be taken.

An idea is a fragile thing. It must be given as much care as any other fragile and precious thing. If we visualize how an ideally inviting school can be and invite others to join our efforts, positive powerful changes can be made. We must start somewhere, see how things are going, adjust as needed, and then sustain the spirit. In order to keep inviting ideas alive and active, attention will be given to them. It is an accepted truth that "What you think about, you bring about." For that reason, every opportunity will be taken to keep the idea of creating an inviting school in the forefront of people's thoughts. When this happens, people will be practitioners of the tenets they have been taught.

People will persevere through rainy periods of life. No one is perfect; therefore, it is necessary for the school family to bond together and remind each other of the importance of the cause beyond themselves of which they are a part. When someone forgets the mission, others will be there to gently remind him or her of the importance of the inviting way. Adopting the motto of "the way we do things around here" in an Inviting School, provides the opportunity for your school to become the most inviting place in town.

Purkey suggests that the secret of the castle is "making it look easy." To me this is like the fine athlete, musician, or dancer who can do incredible feats only because of years of sustained effort and hard work. When they perform, the things they do seem effortless and natural, but the underlying "secret" to their success consists of the years of dedication required to reach that level of achievement.

The importance of establishing a legacy of caring and sustaining the spirit of Invitational education was recently brought home to me. Twenty years ago I went to Grand Heights Early Childhood Center as principal; and now, two decades later, my grandson, Addison, is attending kindergarten there. The Grand Heights staff worked for several years before we were ready to nominate our school for the Inviting School Award. I remember that somewhere in the process, Purkey said, "When are you going to nominate your school for the Inviting School Award?" and I replied, "When we deserve it." I told him that there had been some budget cuts for the following year and that our school was going to be hit hard by the changes. We had to wait to see if we could be "inviting in the rain." With the help of fellow faculty members, parents, and other volunteers, we were able to meet that challenge. In 1987, after five years of intentional effort, our school received the prestigious honor.

Although leaders have come and gone, the inviting spirit has been sustained. The original faculty of that school consciously created a culture of caring and made learning fun and exciting. The stability of that staff and their commitment to the ideals of Invitational education have been the primary reasons for the continued successful implementation of those ideals. This dedicated staff has kept the spirit of invitational education alive and well and they exemplify the attainability of sustaining an inviting school spirit. This has not happened by accident.

Traditions were started and became established as expectations by teachers who recognized the importance of preserving precious practices. The Eager Beaver was synergistically selected as the perfect mascot for a school filled with five-year-olds. The Eager Beaver school song and its positive message is long remembered by students and their parents. I am reminded of a child who came to school several years after its beginning and he told me, "My brother was an Eager Beaver and my sister was an Eager Beaver; and now, I'm an Eager Beaver!!" The sense of belonging to a group is an important need that we all possess. I remember another conversation that I had with a five-year-old child from Grand Heights. He was in my office for fighting on the playground. While describing what had transpired, he sadly stated, "It was just awful, it was Beaver against Beaver." Even at an early age, he knew the need for loyalty to those in his group. Many lessons like these and others that we will never know were learned through the creation of this inviting institution.

It is hard for me to express my excitement about the day I took my grandson to kindergarten orientation. We were both "Eager Beavers" as we went to Grand Heights to see his school and classroom and meet the teachers and principal. I don't know about Addison, but I could hardly sleep the night before. As I lay there thinking of my grandchild starting school, I thought of a story a colleague shared with me. He said that when his daughter started school, she was so excited about the first day that she could not sleep the night before. On the first morning, she ran into the building with boundless enthusiasm. I remembered that next he said, "She was never that excited about school again." It was my prayer that night Addison would always retain his initial Eager Beaver excitement for school and learning and that he would be blessed by caring, conscientious teachers.

Although I have been gone from Grand Heights for many years, I still experienced a warm sense of belonging when Addison and I entered the building. Invitational education is alive and well at Grand Heights Early Childhood Center in Artesia, New Mexico.

As stated earlier, the "secret of the castle" is making it look easy and that is what the staff at Grand Heights does. The teachers there have worked to be the best. Like professional athletes and accomplished musicians, they make it look easy. Yet I know they have honed their skills for years and have intentionally sustained the practice of invitational education and invitational living. My grandson and his friends love school. Although they do not realize the years of intentional effort that has gone into making their school "the most inviting place in town," it is very clear to me.

I was recently given another glimpse of evidence that intentional efforts toward creating inviting schools make a lasting difference. I received a graduation announcement from a former student and accepted the invitation to attend—although the ceremony was many miles from my home. It had been 10 years since Christine was an elementary student at Holloman Primary, but fond memories of her childhood days at our school lingered.

Christine shared a written story of her life with me while I was visiting in her home. After attending kindergarten through second grade at our school; she was transferred to another school where invitational education was not practiced. Tears rolled down my face as I read how a third grade teacher's thoughtless comment caused Christine to quit speaking to anyone other than family members for several years.

Reading the memories of a young person who paused to reflect upon her life, I was reminded of the importance of what we are doing. Teachers touch eternity. We never know how far-reaching our influence will be. This story is shared in hopes of reminding the readers of the importance of intentionality; the importance of thinking about our actions, the importance of realizing that invitational education makes a difference. Making our schools the most inviting place in town is worth the efforts extended. Schools that intentionally exemplify Purkey's and Novak's philosophy of invitational education help to make this world a better place in which to live.

References

Barth, R. S. (1990). *Improving schools from within: teachers, parents and principals can make a difference*. San Francisco: Jossey-Bass.

Novak, J. M. & Purkey, W.W. (2001). *Invitational education*. Fastback 488. Bloomington, IN: Phi Delta Kappa Educational Foundation

Purkey, W. W. & Lehr, J. B. (1991). Invitational education guidebook. *Video Journal of Education, 2*(1), 1-8.

Purkey, W.W., & Novak, J. M. (1996). *Inviting school success, 3ʳᵈ Edition A Self Concept Approach to Teaching, Learning and Democratic Practice*. New York: Wadsworth.

Chapter 3

The Calcium
Primary School Story

Wendy Rocca, Harvey Smith, and Lana Taylor

Behind the water tower of Calcium, New York, nestled between a military base and a cow pasture, is one of the best-kept secrets in education. Here you will find plenty of smiling faces, happy children, excited parents who participate in school life, teachers and support staff acting as coaches and mentors, and people from the community who are frequent visitors to this inviting school in action.

The Calcium Primary School story begins way back, approximately thirty years ago, when Dr. Harvey Smith, professor of education at the State University of New York at Potsdam, created a course on "Developing a Positive Self Concept." The invitational education model was promoted, it was lived, and much excitement was built around this concept. Some twenty years later a teacher from Calcium Primary School, Debbie Reddick, attended one of Harvey's classes. Debbie was selected as part of a Leadership Team, which was comprised of one teacher from each grade level, a special education teacher, head teacher, and a principal. This team was starting a brand new school and their job was to help develop a philosophy and a mission statement for Calcium Primary School.

They began by discussing their beliefs and attitudes toward children and education. It was through this discussion that Debbie realized that what she was hearing was in fact exactly what she had just read and heard about in her class with Harvey Smith. She ran down to her new classroom to get a Phi Delta Kappa Fastback to share with her colleagues. They found themselves very excited and eager to begin their school around the concepts of invitational education.

About a year later, the Head Teacher, Diane Recupero, asked Harvey if he would come and speak with their staff on the Fastback—"Education by Invitation Only" (Purkey & Novak, 2001). Diane discussed these ideas and concepts with her principal, Lana Taylor, who was really encouraged and bought a copy of this book for each member of her staff with the goal of "intentionally" implementing and embodying theses concepts throughout Calcium Primary School and the surrounding educational community.

Another year went by and Harvey started to receive phones calls from the teachers at Calcium inviting him to stop by and see how the new school was progressing and to witness all the great and exciting things that were happening. For the next three or four summers Harvey began to notice that many other teachers from Calcium School were taking his course on "Self Concept." The Calcium team continued to grow with the complete support and encouragement of their principal, Lana Taylor.

Lana was a true leader who was forthright and had a clear vision for creating an inviting school. Harvey would visit the school from time to time and offer his support and encouragement. At that time Calcium was the only school Harvey found to be entirely intentionally inviting. "Nothing was off limits. The teachers and administers worked as a team and were open to any change needed to make this school the most inviting place in town!" said Harvey. The school welcomes all visitors with a beautiful atrium full of trees, plants, and important and significant works that the children create and value. Harvey says, "it feels like a breath of fresh air and a new era for all those that learn and grow here, like the way it is suppose to be."

Harvey loved this wonderful place so much that he told them

he was going to recommend them for the inviting school award. The team was so excited about this opportunity, but Harvey made Lana promise that if she won the award she would have to go to Virginia Beach and receive the award in person. So in Lana's style she said "Harvey, if we win the award, I'll bring my whole school down there." The deal was made.

The school went all out to win the inviting school award. According to Harvey Smith, their presentation book is a "classic." They did everything exactly right, with no short cuts. In the meantime, Lana started an "Invitation Education Budget" for special events. These special funds did not come out of the district budget. Lana and her staff found creative ways to earn money, through car washes, bake sales, auctions and other innovative events for special occasions.

Calcium won the inviting school award due to their exceptional work and Lana was determined to bring the entire school to participate in this honor. The school had been raising money for an event just like this, so it was decided they would rent a bus and they would *all* head down to Virginia Beach to pick up this special award. On Friday afternoon staff, students, bus drivers, maintenance staff, and volunteers went to school with their suitcases packed and were looking forward to their very long journey. It was an exciting time, they sang, they laughed, and they slept very little. Harvey was sound asleep in the hotel in Virginia Beach. At about 6:00 a.m. he knew the Calcium team had arrived because he was disturbed by a lot of happy noise and a whole lot of cheerful fanfare.

On Saturday afternoon Calcium School was honored with the Inviting School Award. The teachers, students, and support staff came forward to receive their award. In true Calcium style, they were prepared with a song that was written and composed by two of their teachers. The song was called "Lift Them Up," which they sang in two-part harmony. Harvey refers to this wonderful song as a piece of love. There was barely a dry eye in the place, remembers Harvey.

Smith and Novak believe that Calcium Primary School is a school that walks the walk, talks the talk, and rides the road to success. Harvey Smith is so proud of this school that he now teaches his course on "Developing a Positive Self-Concept" every summer at Calcium Primary School so his students can see, learn, and enjoy the inviting environment that Calcium School provides to all those who eagerly enter their doors.

Interview with Lana Taylor:
The Leader with a Vision

Lana, the principal from Calcium School agreed to an interview to discuss her journey on how she was able to create an inviting school that supports learning, enthusiasm, and hope for all those who come in contact with her school.

Background

Lana has been in the education profession for approximately thirty-five years, during which she has gained diversified knowledge and skill. For several years she was an administrator in the state of Colorado and then gave up her position to travel overseas with her spouse who was serving in the military at that time. Her new position in Germany put her right back in the classroom where she taught a class of grade 5 students and a class of grade 6 students. During this period of time she was able to step back from her role as an administrator and gain a deeper appreciation for what teachers were going through and came away with a greater understanding of what the essential issues were within the classroom on a daily basis. Within two years, Lana's spouse was again transferred, and this time her home became Fort Drum in Calcium, New York. Within a very short time, her knowledge, skill, and experience put her right back in the position of administrator. So, in 1991, Lana accepted the position of principal at the newly built Calcium Primary School.

Lana felt very fortunate to participate in the opening of Calcium Primary School. All of the students would transfer from other schools within the district. Her teaching team consisted of approximately ninety percent of teachers who transferred from other schools within the district and a very small selection of new hires who were willing to make a commitment, take a risk, and had the energy to start all over again. She understood that she could not take all the top teachers of the district because they had to create a balance and keep strong all the schools throughout the entire community.

Becoming a Leader

Early in Lana's life she was fortunate to work with some great educators and believes she is where she is today because of them. Lana learned to take her mentorship seriously and strongly encourages others to do the same. In fact, all of her teachers have mentors until they are tenured.

Over the years, Lana has picked up many strategies and bits and pieces of information, some good and some not so good. She feels it is just as valuable to know what to do as it is to know what not to do. She believes that successful people surround themselves with successful people who share the same vision, goals, and mission.

Lana learned early on that she needed people to create things, as one cannot create great things alone. She believes that titles do not mean anything unless you have strong people around you who can help support and build on your work and create dynamic synergies. Lana has no use for leaders who deem themselves "powerful," as they usually have dictatorial type of thinking, believing they have all the answers and spend most of their time telling people what to do. Lana has worked with people who showed her that the way to create success is for people to give you power. You can't take power, you must earn it through respect, and then people will give you their time and energy and help you to create something wonderful.

Vision

Lana knew that the main reason for the existence of Calcium Primary School was to serve the children of Fort Drum, a military base consisting of approximately thirty thousand troops and family members. Many people are there for only a few years and off they go to somewhere else to create a new life. But Lana's dream was to create an inviting school where children and parents always felt welcomed, as if it were their second home. One-third of the school's population turns over within a year as eighty-five percent of the students are from military families. Lana understood that many of her students lived far away from their family members, friends, and loved ones. She knew this could be a very lonely existence and her desire was to create a community within her school that felt like a second home where all children could feel safe, secure, and cared for. She wanted to create a warm, loving, and caring environment for all her children.

Lana decided to establish a communications team that consisted of a representative from each grade level, a representative from the special areas, a representative from special education, and a representative from the support staff to develop new strategies for the school. This team spent a lot of time brainstorming and a member of the team suggested that they take a look at Harvey Smith's work and review a little book entitled *Education: By Invitation Only* (Purkey & Novak, 1988). The connection was made, their philosophy was established, their roadmap was in place. They built their school around the invitational model. After twelve years of hard work, the solid foundation of the invitation model still remains the cornerstone of Calcium Primary School.

Because the school has a very high percentage of students associated with the military, Calcium Primary School has been richly rewarded with a "rainbow" of multiculturalism and skill levels. At every opportunity this school celebrates the students' differences and similarities and honors their many heritages and traditions. The entire community is encouraged to participate in this celebration of people, which promotes tolerance, acceptance, and inclusion. Obstacles and barriers are removed, which allow for an open environment where honest communication and dialogue can take place.

Each morning before school begins all students and staff say the Pledge of Allegiance and then recite the Calcium Pledge that states, "I pledge to respect myself and others, I pledge to make a positive difference in this world as a Calcium peacemaker." The pledge was written because the staff at Calcium Primary School believes that all people count and everyone has value.

Peacemaking is an important part of the program at Calcium school and students learn to resolve their conflicts in a productive way. When peacemaking is required, the students put on their hard hats and are reminded to sit at the peace table where conflict can be resolved through dialogue and hard work. They are supported with a peacemaking toolbox that has all the tools they need to come to a resolution: a compass, a bottle of whiteout, and a magnifying glass. The compass reminds students that they are headed in the right direction, the bottle of whiteout reminds them to forgive themselves as well as others, and the magnifying glass allows them to look at the problem clearly. This school believes that if they treat people with dignity and respect, they can expect no less from others. Lana believes that when the students are respectful to each other, the quality of education in the classroom rises to a new and higher level. Calcium students learn very quickly that hands are for helping, not hurting, and are reminded that they are peace ambassadors. Peace training also provides an invaluable life-skill for future conflict resolution. Because of the military background of most of the children from Calcium, it is a reality that many of these children may be deployed to many different countries and it is Lana's hopes that when the children leave her school that they will become peacemakers throughout the world.

Educating the Educator

This team makes things happen. When there are budget cutbacks, they look for different kinds of opportunities and they have discovered that sometimes the wealth of knowledge they are searching for is within oneself. Cooperative learning among children holds true for teachers as well. Every week, on their own time, the teachers come in early in the morning and take turns presenting a chapter in a book. "It is so wonderful to see our teachers learning from each other. They are proud to share their information, strategies, and knowledge. Everyone is asking questions and learning," said Lana. On a regular basis her teachers present workshops on invitational education to other interested educators. We can do so many great things for ourselves and so many great things for our children, is a motto that Lana lives by. The people at Calcium school also believe if they first honor and take care of themselves, then they have the strength and can care for and honor others. They build their communication on trusting relationships. They care deeply for their fellow colleagues and spend time celebrating and encouraging their successes and achievements.

Difficulty and Conflicts

During our lives, things happen that we learn from. We learn to endure all kinds of stresses. Lana has a profound belief that teaching should be one of the most honored professions in the world and she feels proud to be part of the educational community. She knows she has a difficult job to do and that it does not end at a particular part of the day. Teachers have the kind of job where they have the responsibility of developing or creating good or bad. Lana says that often we don't understand how our actions affect the lives of children that we touch. Everyday as we walk into the classroom, we have an opportunity to make or break a child. We are really teaching the next generation and creating the future. The lessons we impart upon our children are extremely important. We know that we do make a difference. We believe that each child and parent makes a difference. We are successful as educators, as parents, and as human beings because we take one child, one association at a time, and that makes for a good place to work and live or a bad place to work and live.

At the beginning of each year Lana says to all staff, "What if it were your child in this school?" Every decision you make, everything you say, think of the way you want your child treated. Put yourself in the parent's place. We all love our children and want our children to have the best the world can offer. It is vitally important to treat every child with respect and dignity.

When teachers are not showing the commitment that is expected, Lana tries extremely hard to work with them, although she admits there were times she had to let some go because she values children too much to allow inadequacy. She believes in giving people a chance and she has found that there have been very few times in her career where a person could not be mentored, taught, and coached to improve their performance.

Lana knows her teachers. When her teachers are having difficulties she realizes that they are usually having challenges in their personal life. She tries to understand their difficulties and find resources to help them out. She models her expected behavior and the minute she walks into the doors of Calcium school she begins her day by putting a smile on her face and expects all her staff to do the same. She believes being filled with anger and with frustration makes it difficult do justice for children.

Lana has learned during difficult times to stand back, take a deep breath, and realize it is just something you have to go through. She does not take it personally, which she says, is one of the hardest lessons to learn in life. She believes that if you keep all the negative feelings inside you, you are not going to be able to do the job effectively and successfully. She says just "let water roll off your back and do not internalize it." She understands that there are lots of pressures in all our lives, but she believes that if we learn our lessons, learn from our mistakes and find new and better ways of doing things, trust in ourselves, and make decisions in good faith, then things usually work out. Sure there are times, she said, that she may have been able to do things better, so she learns her lesson and does things differently the next time around.

Inviting School Award

Lana believed that the Inviting School Award was the most important award of her career. She took the honor very seriously and prepared for everyone to enjoy the fruits of their labor. She wanted everyone to feel proud of all they accomplished together as a community. They worked hard at raising funds to attend the awards ceremony where they performed their special song entitled,

"Lift Them Up" that was written for this special occasion. It was a real honor and one she will cherish for a lifetime.

Keeping the Dream Alive

Calcium Primary School also has their own school theme song that was written by two teachers and the students sing it at every assembly and every chance they get. The students, teachers, and parents feel like they are a part of a special community and they let people know who they are and what they are all about. They spend time developing and nurturing their image and promoting all the good things happening in this inviting atmosphere. Calcium Primary School has created a brochure to let people know that they have a wonderful place to be discovered. They are currently in the process of creating a website to enhance their image and reputation. Still Lana feels that word of mouth is the most effective advertising of all. Often the local television station will call looking for good news because they love the school, the celebrations, and the enthusiastic children and teachers.

Lana works hard at getting funds, grants, and other money to strengthen and support her school. She believes if you tell the truth and let people know that you have a good place to educate children, the dream will keep itself alive.

Dr. Kate Asbill, a supporter and friend of Calcium Primary School, believes that all the teachers, students, parents, and volunteers at this school work extremely hard at creating an intentionally inviting school. Kate says that when you walk into the school it is extremely inviting and you can actually feel the positive energy surrounding you, but she reminds us that people are hard at work creating this environment through their intentional and thoughtful practices. It is only through the intentional thoughtful care of the educators at Calcium Primary School has this school established themselves as the "most inviting place in town."

The Invitational Helix

Calcium Primary School is an "invitational HELIX" (Purkey & Novak, 1996) in action, a spinning vortex of continuous improvement. From the beginning, Lana Taylor and her team recognized the need for a solid education model to build their school. They intuitively chose the "invitational education" model, and agreed as a team, to give it a try. They understood how the foundational principles functioned and continued to work together through trial and error, making adjustments along the way. It wasn't until they attended Harvey Smith's workshop on "Developing a Positive Self Concept" that they really begin to develop a profound understanding and insight on the power of applying the invitational education philosophy. This team of teachers was so determined to create the "most inviting place in town" that they made a firm commitment and adopted the invitational education principles necessary to succeed in an intentionally inviting way.

Throughout the stages of development and progression, Calcium Primary School continues to refine and improve their processes of creating an inviting school. They continue to define what their inviting educational community should look and feel like. They are creating their own inviting future and encouraging others to come along, but most importantly, they are providing a promising future for every child that is lucky enough to participate in this special place called "Calcium Primary School."

Conclusion

After visiting this school myself in the summer of 2003 I was able to observe that all the teachers within this school were passionate about their work and the environment that they created for their students and for themselves. I concluded that it is not enough to have an inviting school theory, or well-trained teachers, or a brand new school with the latest technology, or outstanding curriculum. What makes this school different is that these talented people intentionally weave their education, training, beliefs, and values into their work, and the total sum of all the many parts have created a magic that is called an "inviting school." These people who come together each morning with a purpose to teach, mentor, and coach students and themselves, have what Novak refers to as an intentional love of live life. They continually invite themselves, as well as others to participate in a thoughtful and intentional educational life. They believe in themselves, they believe in others, and, most importantly, they believe in their work. They are happy to share their successes and pass on their knowledge, experiences, and skills to others, for they believe that all schools should be built on the invitational model as it invites success for all those who have the courage to begin the journey. Lana won't tell you that this process is easy, but she will tell you that each day her team takes risks and has the courage to keep on trying. They continue to look for innovative and creative ways to create an inviting school for each child. The members of the educational community of Calcium Primary School take pride and are rewarded as they watch their children learn, grow and develop. This principal, her teachers, support workers, maintenance people, and bus drivers all continue to make a valuable contribution to society daily and their hope is that their children will do the same. These educators know and understand that their contribution to children today will shape and contribute to a better tomorrow.

References

Novak, J. M. & Purkey, W.W. (2001). *Invitational education.* Fastback 488. Bloomington, IN: Phi Delta Kappa Educational Foundation.

Purkey, W.W., & Novak, J. M. (1996). *Inviting school success, 3rd Edition: A self concept approach to teaching, learning, and democratic practice.* New York: Wadsworth Publishing.

Chapter 4

Inviting News
from St. John Neumann School

Barbara Cole

How does a school go from an enrollment of 59 to over 390 in just fourteen years? With a lot of hard working, dedicated people, and absolute faith, that's how.

St. John Neumann Parish purchased Wildewood School in 1985 as a means to increase its education base within the parish. This new school offered classes from kindergarten through grade twelve to only 59 students. After a period of time, it became apparent that things were not proceeding according to plan. Enrollment continued to decline yearly, until Wildewood School became a "financial burden" to the parish. The school had to be more inviting, but how? In 1988, the parish decided to hire a new principal and change the name of the school to St. John Neumann School, indicating a fresh start and a new beginning.

Under the principalship of Dr. Margaret Adams, the pastor, Father Fredrick Masad, and the Bishop of the Diocese, it was decided that St. John Neumann School would become a school offering kindergarten through to second grade, increasing one grade each year as required by the community.

The school was completely renovated. All the classrooms were painted in bright cheerful colors, new carpets were installed and long needed repairs were made. Dr. Adams called upon parents, community members, and parishioners to join her during the summer to complete the work for the grand opening. One could feel the atmosphere of excitement and anticipation waiting for the students to arrive in September.

In the fall of 1989, St. John Neumann School opened its doors to welcome 100 students who would enter and participate in this new environment that encouraged school success. Thus, the motto of the school became "*Experience Success.*" The first day was filled with fun and excitement. The students were welcomed to the "new" school by the colorful paintings of kites, balloons, and other eye appealing motifs. The hard work, support, and dedication of the volunteers that summer spilled over to the hard work, excitement, and dedication of the students that first year and continue to this day. This was the real beginning of St. John Neumann School in Columbia, South Carolina.

Parents have always been an intricate part of St. John Neumann School. In fact, they are encouraged to participate on a regular basis and their presence is felt every day and in every facet of our school life. Parents are involved as morning greeters, helpers in the Discovery Center, the library, the cafeteria, the office, and of course, the classrooms. Parent volunteers can be found planning and implementing such school activities as "Family Night," where a casual picnic dinner encourages families to get to know each other as they listen to performances by the children. There is also the Halloween Carnival, Field Day, and the annual fundraisers: "The Annual Fund" and the Auction. The Auction is our major fundraiser that involves a silent/live auction, where the community donates items to be auctioned. However, the largest "winnings" comes from the items made by the students and vied for by their parents. We also have a mentor program that helps new students and their families become acquainted with the school, its policies, and for all new families moving into Columbia. A real sense of ownership and belonging can be felt throughout the school as the parents contribute to this successful environment.

We live our school motto, *"Experience Success,"* daily. Before the school day begins, the students take turns presenting the morning news show that is televised in each classroom. The students lead everyone in our morning prayers, the Pledge of Allegiance, and inspirational thoughts for the day. We then recite the Pledge of Honor, which states:

> As a St. John Neumann Student, I will show respect for myself and others at all times. I will honor my work and the work of others. I will show integrity and honor in all my accomplishments. And I will treat all I meet with the kindness of Jesus.

After the news show, our academic day begins. Discipline is not an issue at our school as our students are expected to behave in a civilized, well-mannered way, and they do. We continually emphasize living by the standards established in the "Golden Rule". Our student body consistently surpasses the Diocesan goals on standardized national and state testing. Students cheerfully great others as they pass in the hall. They take a great deal of pride in their school and are often seen picking up a piece of paper and putting it in the trash or bending to pick up and re-hang an example of student work that has fallen from the wall.

Only a dedicated faculty and staff could facilitate such a successful program, and ours is such a staff. Teachers frequently work in small groups or with individuals during their own planning time or lunchtime. The faculty is required to offer one afternoon a week to work with students who need special attention; however, everyday finds teachers staying long past their "going home time" to meet with parents, tutor individuals or groups, give cram sessions prior to a big test, or just listening to those who want to talk.

In recognition of the hard work of the faculty, staff, parents, and student body of St. John Neumann School, our school received the 1999 National Blue Ribbon for Academic Excellence Award.

In 2001, the leadership of St. John Neumann School changed to Mrs. Barbara Cole. Mrs. Cole, the new principal, brought many years experience and knowledge with her to the school. She continues to maintain the high standards and morals that had been put in place. She can be seen daily walking the halls, greeting both parents and students, commenting about how well a student has done on an assignment, or congratulating one for finally making the grade that student had been striving for on a particularly test. Most of the student work comes across Mrs. Cole's desk. She writes comments on every test taken by our students, making her very knowledgeable and able to comment to each student about his/her progress.

Teachers send monthly newsletters home from each class to keep immediate family members informed of all events and exciting classroom activities. However, many years ago, we recognized that we needed a vehicle to spread the good news of St. John Neumann to a wider community. As luck would have it, some of our parents volunteered to design and create a newsletter for our school. These parents also went out into the community to seek support and assistance through advertising funds to make our newsletter something very special. From their hard work, the *Eagle Events* was developed. It started out as a typical school newsletter, being copied and stapled, then distributed. With time, we were blessed to have parents with the expertise of being graphic artists. That is when the newsletter developed into what we have today. Our community newsletter includes information from our Principal, Parent School Association President, School Board President, and a variety of other articles written by parents, teachers, and even students. These articles run the gamut from school and classroom activities, ongoing service projects, to favorite recipes. Today, our popular newsletter is mailed to over 1,000 households monthly—families, friends, alumni, and grandparents enjoy keeping up with our successes.

Mrs. Cole brought with her a more formalized approach to invitational education, and our school began to evaluate itself through the lens of that assessment. Committees were formed and the philosophies of people, place, policies, procedures, and programs were implemented. In 2002, St. John Neumann School was awarded the International Inviting School Award by the International Alliance of Invitational Education. In October, while Mrs. Cole led a delegation to Atlanta to receive the International Inviting School Award, the parents and children were having a day of celebration of their own back in Columbia. Everyone was justifiably proud of this accomplishment as we are now the only school in the Diocese to have received the National Blue Ribbon and an Inviting School Award.

The unique feature that makes St. John Neumann School the shining star that it is today is the involvement and dedication of all involved. Our students do not enter the doors alone; their families enter with them. Families, students, faculty, and staff become a school family committed to the vision of St. John Neumann School. We all work in concert to assure continued excellence at our school.

So how does a school go from an enrollment of 59 to over 390 in just 14 years? The answer is, a solid vision, strong leadership, a lot of hard work, and a multitude of dedicated people who believe all things are possible.

Chapter 5

Caring, Communication, and Collaboration:
A Director of Teacher Development's Perspective

Sue Bowen

Never doubt that a small group of thoughtful, committed citizens can change the world. Indeed, it is the only thing that ever has.

Inviting Schools don't just happen. They are created by caring, thoughtful people who have developed their skills in communication and team building. They are sustained by staff working together in a collaborative fashion with frequent discussions of the importance of putting invitational theory into creative and supportive practices. In my experiences as a Teacher, Professional Development Coordinator, and Assistant Superintendent of Curriculum and Instruction, I have seen small groups of staff members start a study of invitational education in their work setting that ultimately changes the climate of the entire school or district in a positive way. Usually someone in the group has read a book about invitational education or has heard someone speaking on the topic. The enthusiasm of one individual will spark the interest of one or two colleagues. As the concept of invitational education is explored and discussed by two or more, other colleagues note their enthusiasm. If it did not start with the building principal, it soon will catch his/her attention.

That is the beginning, and so begins the opportunity for a small group of staff members to change the school! I watched the transformation of Enslow Middle School in Huntington, West Virginia, after a team of four teachers attended an international conference for invitational education. The teachers returned from the conference full of ideas that would help them lead their school to be one of the 1990 International Alliance for Invitational Education (IAIE). Award winning schools. Enslow was an older building, but it took on a fresh look with rooms painted cheerful colors and plants and mirrors added to the hallways. In all the halls and classrooms, student work was displayed. The school rules were rewritten in positive terms and the teachers made a concentrated effort to communicate with parents on a regular basis. The Enslow team conducted monthly meetings and invited representatives from the other seven middle schools in the district. The meetings were designed to share inviting strategies and success stories. My role as Director of Curriculum and Staff Development for the Cabell County District, in Huntington, West Virginia, was to listen, support, and encourage. I was quite impressed with how much influence this team of four teachers had on their school and their school district.

In 1993, when I moved to Kentucky to take the position of Assistant Superintendent of Curriculum and Instruction of Woodford County, I knew I wanted to introduce the concepts of invitational education to the six schools in Woodford County in the same way the four teachers of Enslow had shared the ideas with their school and district.

Since then, I have been involved with schools and districts that stayed the course and have used invitational education as the foundation for all decisions and all school improvement efforts. These particular schools provide an enjoyable work environment. Further, students and staff look forward to coming to school, and parents want their children to attend such learning environments. These are schools where each student is valued and parents are partners in the educational process. These are the inviting schools.

Five of the six schools in Woodford County earned the status of being designated an Inviting School by IAIE during my service to the district. Southside Elementary School led the way with a thorough study of invitational education. The principal and teams of Southside teachers did multiple invitational education workshops in Kentucky. This school was recognized as an invitational School in 1995. Three other elementary schools, Northside, Huntertown and Simmons earned the Inviting School Award in 1998. In 2000, Woodford County Middle School earned this distinction.

Educators from these Award Schools formed an invitational education cadre with representatives from three other districts in central Kentucky. Fayette County, Jessamine County, Scott County, and Woodford County collaborated to sponsor the 1998 IAIE World Conference in Lexington, Kentucky. All four districts have had success with their invitational education initiatives. The collaboration and sharing among these four districts helped the members of the IE cadre to adopt invitational thinking in their personal and professional lives.

Fayette County, including Lexington, is the second largest district in Kentucky. This district began an internal IE Award project and schools in the district cooperated and shared strategies to make schools more inviting for students, staff, and parents. Members of the IE Cadre from the other districts did school visits and reviewed the Inviting Checklist with Fayette Schools. Two of the schools in Fayette County, Johnson Elementary and Southern Elementary, earned the International Award in 2000. Jessamine County used invitational education as criteria to judge all projects and programs for their school system. All staff members were trained in IE philosophy and they continue to have IE training as an integral part of their school improvement efforts. Two schools in Jessamine County, Wilmore Elementary (1998) and The Early Learning Village (2002), have been named Inviting Schools. Scott County hosted a Quality Circle International Conference in the summer of 2002 and they included invitational education as one of four strands of this conference. Through their involvement with

IAIE, they have developed a partnership with invitational educators in Hong Kong and have developed an exchange program for staff and students. Scott County has three schools that have received the prestigious IAIE Inviting School Award. Southern Elementary earned this recognition in 1998, Northern Elementary received the Award in 2000 and the Scott County Ninth Grade School was so honored in 2002. The collaboration of educators from these four districts helped each district with their invitational goals. It was my privilege to work with these wonderful student centered schools.

Where do we begin the process of introducing the philosophy of Invitational thinking in a school or district?

We begin by meeting as a staff and reviewing our shared vision for the school or the district. We review our belief that all people have the ability and desire to learn. If anyone has any doubts on this, they are asked to "act" as though they believe it, until their thoughts can be transformed. To paraphrase Margaret Mead, a small group of dedicated staff members can influence an entire staff to strive to make their school "the most inviting place in town." Here are specific steps that you take to lead a school on the invitational journey.

Step One:
Introduce Invitational Education
as a Way of Thinking and Doing

A critical mass of teachers and staff personnel should review the basics of invitational education. This group should meet with the building administrator and discuss the merits of a thorough study of the research and literature available pertaining to invitational education. Involve the Professional Development committee. Together, decide how the information about invitational education should be presented to the entire staff.

Personally, I found it helpful to meet with team members frequently, for short periods of time, whether the team be the Curriculum Staff, or the Academic Coaches, or the Extended School Services Representative, etc. Face to face communication is essential for solid team building. At each meeting, there should be some reference to some time devoted to, a discussion of the shared vision or mission of the group. The commonly developed Mission Statement can be posted, printed, and shared a variety of ways. It can be revisited and modified. A shared vision is essential. As we look at what be believe to be the mission of the school, (or the group you are involved with), we must recognize the reality that there are students and staff members who are disenfranchised and are underachieving. The mission of the school needs to address this reality and share a vision that all will be successful. The mission and goals of a school reflect the desire to grow in invitational education ways to achieve the desired results. The qualities of all staff meetings and team meetings reflect the qualities of invitational education.

As part of the introduction, staff members are given books or articles about invitational education to read. Staff members are encouraged to share their insights with their colleagues. Everyone in the school is informed of the invitational education Website. Knowledge about IE is the foundation for building a truly invitational climate that permeates the entire school environment. Learning and questioning is the beginning of the journey to school improvement.

Step Two:
Establish Ground Rules
for all Meetings in Your School

At the first meeting of the year, the group leader should establish the ground rule expectations of how the meetings will function. Included in the ground rules for every meeting are the qualities of invitational education:

Respect

Respect means to consider worthy of high regard; hence, to refrain from interfering with; to treat with propriety or consideration. For this quality to permeate a building or a system, it must start with the leaders and be modeled at every meeting or event where two or more come together.

Trust

Trust is a confidence in the reliability of persons or things without careful investigation. It is important to develop a meeting atmosphere where participants feel safe to take risks. Trust may take longer to establish than respect, especially if there are members of the group who have difficulty with developing confidence in their peers and colleagues.

Optimism

Optimism involves an inclination to put the most favorable construction upon actions and events or anticipate the best possible outcome. Even as the group studies all sides of an issue, there needs to be the understanding that they will take the best possible action to improve the quality of the school.

Intentionality

Intentionality a settled direction on the mind, toward doing of a certain act. This means done by design; intended. There is an expectation that all people in the school will be intentionally inviting with themselves and others, personally and professionally.

Throughout my career as an educator, I frequently observed the positive accomplishments of face-to-face communication. It is essential that meetings are well organized. The group leader must be sensitive to the scheduled time allotted for the meeting. The participants know the agenda for the meeting and are willing to stay focused on the goals for this time together. If you hear complaints about too many meetings, this is a clue that the meetings are not productive and assisting with the work of the school. When meetings are organized, fun, and productive, participants appreciate the opportunity to work together.

I believe it is important to have regularly scheduled, short, and to the point meetings for every group that has a responsibility for school improvement. However, even when the meeting is short and focused, there should be a relaxed atmosphere and a time to listen to one another. I believe in establishing a starting time and an ending time so that people can plan their days. That is, modeling respect for time and all the responsibilities that come to those working in schools. It is important to build trust by involving each member of the group in making a meaningful contribution to the group's success. The leader's enthusiasm and optimism for group projects and activities must be explicit. The focus for each decision and each plan of action should be designed to benefit our students, our schools, and our community. Someone in the group should verbalize the intentionality of the group's efforts to keep the focus on student and staff success.

Step Three:
Develop a Critical Mass of Staff Devoted
to the Concepts of Invitational Education

You may have two or three teachers who have attended an international conference for invitational education. Or maybe, there are a couple of teachers in your school who have heard a bit about invitational education and decided to read a book or two on the topic. Now what?

This is the beginning of developing a critical mass of teachers who will support the concept of invitational learning and teaching. Encouragement to these teachers can come in a variety of ways. These teachers need encouragement. First, be an active listener. Find out what improvements they want to focus on in the beginning. Second, provide them with support by giving them time and resources to be successful in the designated improvements. This is also the time for the school leader to be intentionally inviting professionally by providing these teachers opportunities to share at department meetings or grade level meetings.

Perhaps you are a new principal to a school and no one there has even heard of invitational education, William W. Purkey, or

Betty L. Seigel! Now what? I suggest you order five or six copies of the PDK Fastback, *Invitational Education*, by Novak and Purkey (2001). Choose three or four teacher leaders and one or two leaders in the classified work force. Invite them to meet with you and give them a copy of the Invitational Education Fastback and ask them to read it and set a meeting for a week later. When you meet a second time, spend thirty minutes or more listening to their reaction to what they have read. This is an effective way to develop a core group of supporters to introduce invitational education to the entire staff.

You may be a teacher who believes in the principles of IE and you want others on the staff to develop an understanding of the invitational philosophy. I encourage you to gain the support of the principal of your school. The principal is truly the Instructional Leader who sets the tone and lends the support the school needs to transform to an invitational environment. It is appropriate for you to request professional development training that focuses on invitational teaching and learning.

Whatever your situation, you can make a difference in your circle of influence. As a teacher, you can change your classroom so that you model invitational thinking in every action you take. If you are the school secretary, the office can become a place that is inviting to students, parents, and the community. If you are the school custodian, the pride you take in making the school clean and attractive and the pleasant interchanges of communication you have with students can make your department inviting to all. If you are a committee chair, you can model invitational thinking in how you conduct meetings. If you are school principal, cafeteria worker, or teacher's aide, you can make a difference by internalizing the philosophy of invitational education and modeling it in all your actions and interactions.

Step Four:
Build a Solid Foundation
with a two-year Professional Development Plan
for Invitational Education

A two-year professional development plan is developed so that there is an ongoing study of invitational education. This can be done though monthly study groups, independent reading, traditional IE workshops, or a combination of all three methods. I would caution you against setting a tone that conveys that this is a TYNT project. (This Year's New Thing). Instead the study should be integrated into ongoing work in curriculum development or the School Improvement Plan.

Effective professional development forms a foundation that models the excitement of learning for adults. Many schools have moved from stand and deliver workshops. Specifically, schools now give opportunities for individuals to read, to form study groups, and to personally select training based on the individual needs an interests. Creative leaders have designed individual plans that encourage teachers and staff members to far exceed the individual's contracted required number of hours for Professional Development. In these districts, teachers are recognized for their commitment to learning. Many districts have altered their week schedule to allow students to go home at noon, one day a week, so that teachers have one half day a week built into their schedule for professional growth activities. Some principals use part of each staff meeting for professional growth and development. There are a variety of ways to find time for the entire staff to develop an in-depth understanding of what is meant by invitational education and how this understanding can lead to a changed environment that summons each individual to develop intellectually, socially, physically, psychologically and spiritually.

Staff development cannot consist of one workshop prior to the start of the school year, or one speech by an outside consultant or a visit to an IE Award School. These may be desirable, and worthwhile to help develop a common language about invitational learning and teaching, but a one-time experience cannot provide a variety of IE activities and learning experiences that are needed for invitational education to flourish. During the first year, the IE plan is monitored and adjusted to meet the needs of the school/staff. At the end of the second year, a new two-year plan is developed to stay the course.

One of the professional development activities that I found to be particularly helpful was to have a five-day Teacher's Academy that focuses on invitational education during the summer months. You can study in depth and have a lot of fun devising invitational strategies that can be used in the classrooms when school opens for students. Just as it is true with students, teachers also need to hear information presented in a variety of ways before it becomes a part of their long-term memory. The two year professional development plan will help with the development of a common IE vocabulary for all staff members. Developing a common language is an ongoing process that can be enhanced by the work that is done in the organization to apply invitational thinking to the five P's. For a school to be viewed as inviting to the internal and external publics, it takes all the adults in the school working together to achieve an atmosphere that is truly inviting.

Step Five:
Form Five Committees—
People, Place, Policies, Processes, and Programs

Having this structure provides you with the opportunity to reorganize some of the committees you currently have. It is important that staff does not feel this is an "add on" or an extra assignment. The five P's cover all the areas of concern to help staff do the business of school. It is important to help them view this as a new way of looking at the mechanics of a well-run school.

Southern Elementary, in Scott County, Kentucky, formed committees based on the 5 Ps. They eliminated all other committees they had in place. Everything they did in school fits under the category of People, Place, Program, Process, or Policy. Southern Elementary, Scott County expected all staff members serve on a committee. This provides the service personnel with the opportunity to participate in decision making along with teachers and administrators. This staff found they wanted to do a refresher course each year to keep staff focused on the IE ways of doing things and to introduce IE concepts to any new staff members.

Those who serve on the Places Committee will find instant gratification in making visible changes. They will want to add plants to the hallways, clean up the staff lounge area, and review the school signs to be certain they are welcoming. These are positive improvements. It is equally important that they search for attractive ways to display student work and to change these displays frequently. A Student of the Month Bulletin Board helps communicate the priority of the school. This committee will want to include representatives from the custodial staff and the cafeteria staff. The cleanliness of the building and the attractive presentation of the food are important components of an inviting Place.

I suggest the Policy Committee start with a review of the Mission Statement that was discussed earlier in this chapter. They will want to review current policies affecting attendance, homework, discipline, and grading. If there is concern that any policy is not fair to any one member of the school community, this group will revise the policy and present it to the staff for discussion. The policies and procedures need to be consistent throughout the school. For example, if students in one class are sent to the office for being late, while those in another class are not, it sends contradictory messages to the students regarding the expectations of the school. Changing poorly written policies that have been in place for a while presents a real challenge. It is worth the efforts that this committee makes to have inviting polices in all areas of school governance.

The Program Committee will look at current programs and see if they are inclusive. They will look for programs that are needed for the school to meet the needs of the students and staff of the school. The Program Committee may decide there is a need for

Peer Counseling and recommend professional development in that area. They will be involved in broadening parent involvement. They may develop an after school program to give additional assistance to students who need more time to master the curriculum. There is no limit to the variety of programs that may be studied or created to meet the needs of the school.

Sometimes the Processes Committee has difficulty in finding a focus. It seems more abstract than Places, Programs or Policies. This committee concentrates its study not on what we do, but how we do it. Are there a variety of teaching strategies being used in every classroom? Is cooperative learning alive and well in the classroom and collaboration a part of the school culture? This committee makes recommendations to improve the school climate. These recommendations are specific and consistent with invitational thinking.

It could be argued that the Social Committee is the most important committee of the school. You may want to consider forming a People Committee made up of representatives from the other four committees. They can plan the luncheons, and other social times for the staff. This committee helps create a sense of family for the school staff and students.

Step Six:
Monitor Progress

You started by having a vision for what your school should be. You have laid the foundation so that everyone in the school has the basic knowledge of the basic beliefs of invitational education and why the four qualities of IE are essential to creating an Inviting School atmosphere. Those two things have taken some time. I feel it is necessary to remind the reader that this is only the beginning. I have witnessed schools that have this healthy beginning only to move on to study the latest innovation and not allow a continuation of an in-depth study of invitational education. They have studied invitational education and have moved on. When that happens, the school does not reach its full potential and invitational education is not sustained.

One of the best tools you have to stay the course is the Inviting School Checklist. These one hundred statements can be broken into segments of four or ten for study and discussion. The statements can be given to students for their reaction, or to parents for theirs. These reactions can be compared to teacher's perspectives. If any group sees a need for improvement, this should be addressed by the staff. Face to face discussion of the issues raised by studying the one hundred statements of the Inviting School Checklist is vital.

One of many possible ways to use the Checklist is to have each staff member fill one out as you begin the IE journey and record the number or percent of responses under each number beside the item. It is good practice to do the same procedure one year later and compare the scores.

Just as every staff person should be able to articulate the School Mission, each staff person should be able to explain the levels of invitationalism and the importance of the working in all areas of the 5 P's of invitational Learning. Teachers are able to give specific examples of how they have applied invitational education to their classroom management and their instructional strategies. Classified personnel will cite how the training in IE has changed their approach to the work of the school. This common language is essential for checking progress and growth.

Step Seven:
Connect with Other Inviting Schools

As your school becomes increasingly invitational, you will want to explore outside of your immediate school environment to learn what others are doing. Get a list of schools that have earned the IAIE Inviting School Award in recent years. Contact some of these schools and learn what they are doing.

If possible, arrange an exchange visit with a school that has earned the IAIE Award. You have much to share with other schools and much to learn from them. Seeing how others have applied IE in the governance of the school and in the delivery of the curriculum provides a special kind of growth and insight. It affirms what you are doing right and at the same time, you will gather ideas that you will want to apply in your classroom/school.

Give Inviting School Workshops. We all know that one of the best ways to learn something is to teach it. If members of your staff present workshops that share invitational education ideas on a regular basis, the concepts of invitational thinking will be forever embedded in the mind and soul of your school. Consider opportunities to share the message at state and national conferences as well as for other schools within your district. Conduct workshops or mini-presentations for your own staff on a regular basis. Attend the IAIE World Conference with a team from your school. You will gather a variety of strategies that will be wonderful to take back home and share with others on your staff.

Step Eight:
Accentuate the Positive

It is a good idea to bring the entire staff together mid-year for a thirty or forty minute brainstorming session. This is the time to review the five P's of invitational Education with them. A brain storming session with staff having the opportunity to contribute the positives they see about the people of this school is a wonderful way to elevate a mid-year slump. Log these positives on a flip chart or chalkboard. Do this activity with the other four components affected by invitational theory; places, programs, processes and policies. After a time for clarification of all the points made, thank the group for their insights. The results of this brainstorming session should be typed up and circulated to the staff. Each week celebrate one or two of the positives that the staff identified.

Parents are invited to a variety of Open Houses or Curriculum Nights. Parents are made to feel welcome whenever they call or come to the school. An administrator bromide states that what gets monitored, gets done. Keeping track of volunteer hours and then celebrating the volunteers who give so much of their time will encourage more parent participation in the school. A Parent Academy was implemented by Simmons Elementary, Woodford County, Kentucky (Award School, 1998). This was a series of evening sessions that provide parents with a glimpse of their child's daily school life. The teachers taught the curriculum to parents and gave them suggestions on how to help their children with homework assignments. A dinner was served and the Simmons staff met with parents who did not ordinarily come to the school. Other schools in Woodford County had similar programs that gave their schools a chance to show the wonders of their schools.

Creating and sustaining inviting schools is not easy. With caring administrative support, thoughtful communication about the practices to be implemented, and enthusiastic collaboration with parents, community, and other schools, it can be done.

Reference

Novak, J. M. & Purkey, W.W. (2001). *Invitational education*. Fastback 488. Bloomington, IN: Phi Delta Kappa Educational Foundation

Chapter 6

Collaboration through Commitment:
The Garfield Heights Story

Judy Brown Lehr and Ronald Victor

The process of implementing invitational education in a school system may begin at any level. This story details the important role of an innovative leader who was able to transform a school district facing many challenges into a recognized national "model" of invitational education.

The History of Garfield Heights

The road to becoming an inviting school district and community was not easy. In 1992, the Garfield Heights City Schools and the community of Garfield Heights, Ohio, were in disarray. The school district faced a 2.3 million dollar financial deficit and was challenged with a school district transfer issue dividing the community. Test scores were among the lowest in the county and state. Morale and support from the certified and classified staff were at a low point. The community was known as "Garbage Heights" due to a number of landfills that opened in the 1950s and were then closed in the late 1970s. The community had not supported the school district and had failed to approve additional operating funds since the early 1980s. The district was in financial receivership and would soon be at the mercy of the State of Ohio requesting an emergency state loan.

The former superintendent had been terminated by the Board of Education. The Board of Education was viewed by the community as not providing the best educational opportunities for the children attending the public schools. Board members were perceived as having their own personal and political agendas contributing very little leadership as expected by the Ohio School Boards Association Code of Ethics for board members.

The Board of Education faced its biggest challenge, selecting a superintendent who would lead the district despite these most uninviting circumstances. Through the Ohio School Boards Association, the Board of Education conducted a search for its new superintendent. Emerging from the list of candidates was Ronald L. Victor who was employed by a neighboring school district serving as its business manager. On January 1, 1992, Ronald Victor began his position of superintendent. Since that time, the once troubled district has been transformed into a learning community that truly supports education and the principles of invitational education.

Demographic Data

The Garfield Heights Community represents a richly diverse, first-ring suburb of Cleveland, Ohio that is minimally industrial and heavily residential with a population of 32,000. The minority population is 14.42%. The working residents are largely blue collar with an average family income of $28,000.00. Aid to dependent children support is provided to 9.38% of the families. Students in the Garfield Heights City School District come from single parent homes, blended family homes, and two parent homes. Both parents are employed outside of the home in approximately 75% of families with children in the public schools and the parent's general level of education tends to be that of a high school graduate. The public schools currently serve a population of 3,815 students and the parochial and private schools enroll approximately 2500 students in the community.

The Beginning

In 1992, the superintendent called together his first strategic planning meeting. He invited members of the community to come together to rally behind its schools and to help develop a Strategic Plan. Over 300 community-minded individuals came together and volunteered to serve on 14 different strategic planning committees. Emerging from this inviting process, a document titled "Let Success Shine Through" became the guidepost for the district. In addition to being the guidepost, this document lent itself the first theme for the district, "Let Success Shine Through." In November of 1992, the superintendent led a successful campaign to rally the community to approve additional emergency operating funds. Using this infusion of new resources, the district implemented many initiatives developed through the strategic plan, resulting in a renaissance that the district is still enjoying today. Since that time, the strategic plan has been revised three times and today the district has an ambitious Continuous Improvement Plan that focuses on the three priorities: academic goals, the needs of the heart, and appropriate facilities.

The district begins each year with a theme. The theme serves as a catalyst inviting teachers, support staff, administration and the Board of Education to begin the new year with a sense of direction. Since the initial 1992 theme "Let Success Shine Through," other themes have included: 1993 "Success Builds Success," 1994 "A Whole New Pride," 1995 "Never, Ever, Ever, Give up," 1996 "Pride," 1997 "Harmony," 1998 "Results," 1999 "Collaboration Through Commitment," 2000 "Learning for All," 2001 "Improvement", 2002 "Educating the Community—Raising Expectations" and 2003 "Changing for the Future.

The Process

It was in 1999 that I first received a call from Ronald L. Victor inviting me to come and speak to his administrative staff and teach them more on invitational education. I presented the concept of invitational education to 35 energetic administrators, teachers, parents and members of the support staff. I knew then that Garfield Heights was an inviting community.

I was then invited back to present the concepts of invitational education to his entire teaching and support staff. I can still remember that first day when I met the Garfield Heights City Schools staff. The superintendent was at the door greeting every single teacher and support staff member that came into the high school to attend the opening day meeting and breakfast. After his remarks, the superintendent presented each staff member with a t-shirt with the theme "Collaboration Through Commitment" engraved on the sleeve and the Garfield Heights logo on the vest. The atmosphere was so inviting that I felt right at home.

In working with the Garfield Heights Educators, I found a group of individuals deeply committed to the philosophy of invitational education. A notebook was developed for each educator with information on invitational education.

Through lecture and hands-on activities, participants at the seminars were actively engaged in examining the key elements of invitational education, and each school developed a plan to continue to implement the principles of invitational education.

Mission Statement
and Priorities of Garfield Heights

The Garfield Heights learning community demonstrates basic values that meet the needs of the heart with clear academic goals applying to all children in appropriate facilities and where all community members work together.

Deeply rooted within this mission statement are three specific priorities:

Needs of the Heart

The environment in each school is characterized by:

◆ Mutual respect for all people.

◆ A warm, inviting, supportive, and safe atmosphere where adults and students care personally for each other as individuals.

◆ Encouragement of risk-taking without fear of failure.

◆ A sense of family.

Appropriate Facilities

These needs include:

◆ Safe facility conditions.

◆ Renovation and enhancements to existing facilities.

◆ New high school.

Academic Goals

Students demonstrate the ability to:

◆ Read and write at or above grade level.

◆ Do math at or above grade level.

◆ Perform at or above grade level in math, science social studies, and language arts on standardized tests and proficiency tests.

◆ Be healthy, knowledgeable, and contributing citizens.

◆ Think critically and analytically using appropriate criteria to solve real world problems.

◆ Appreciate and/or participate in athletics, the performing arts, the fine arts and/or extracurricular activities.

◆ Work productively in groups with people of various backgrounds.

◆ Communicate effectively both orally and written.

◆ Use personal computers for basic tasks in school, at home, and at work.

Deeply imbedded with the mission and priorities of the Garfield

Heights schools are the ideas of invitational education. Each of the Garfield Heights City school buildings, including Garfield Heights High School, Garfield Heights Middle School, Maple Leaf Intermediate School, William Foster Elementary School, and Elmwood Elementary School have principals, administrative staff, instructional staff and support staff that support the district's priorities, the needs of the heart, appropriate facilities and academic goals.

School employees are very concerned and caring individuals that work very hard to create an environment in their learning community where students feel secure and are dealt with by caring adults. Good discipline is the norm and expectation in all schools.

Schools in the Garfield Heights are more than friendly. Trust, respect, optimism, and intentionality, the ideals of invitational education are promoted each day throughout the school year. The students and teachers are made to feel valuable, capable, responsible, and are expected to grow and flourish within the learning community.

The Garfield Heights City Schools are places where a sense of family is primary. The educational needs, wants, and aspirations of all members of the learning community are considered the district's highest priorities. In each of the Garfield Heights City Schools, visitors are greeted by the smiles of hundreds of students and staff members working together to build a successful educational foundation for each and every student. Through each building's continuous improvement plan, the principles of invitational education are continually examined, modified, and refined.

In addition to meeting the needs of the heart and improving student performance dramatically this year, as demonstrated by the recent student progress on the Ohio Proficiency Tests, administrators, teachers, and students worked in an environment where school construction took place at each school building. Energy enhancements such as window replacement made the schools warmer and more inviting. A new state-of-the-art high school is currently being constructed and scheduled to open in January 2004, and at William Foster Elementary School, a new kindergarten center was completed housing eight kindergarten units, multi-handicapped units and preschool handicapped units serving over 850 students. The learning community of Garfield Heights has truly become a very invitational community facing all the challenges of a typical first ring suburban community of a major Metropolitan City in the United States.

Results

The entire school district has been transformed to an invitational learning community where students flourish. Steady student improvement has been achieved on the annual Ohio Proficiency Test. In 1992, the Garfield Heights City School district scored near the bottom of districts in the State of Ohio. The district has made steady progress and successfully achieved continuous improvement status in February 2002 by meeting additional State standards.

In addition to recently achieving continuous improvement status, the district can boast of tremendous gains in each of the 22 areas that students are assessed. The district's enrollment has jumped from 2875 in 1992 to 3850 today, another sign of an improving learning community. In November of 2000, the community of Garfield Heights passed a $41.5 million bond issue to build both a new high school and renovate and expand each of its district facilities. The residents passed this on the first vote by a 57% margin, and passed an additional $10.5 million bond issue in November 2002 by a 69.3% margin, again a strong sign of a committed community. Another important sign of how this community has become more inviting is the district's Total Community Solution (TCS). The Total Community Solution consists of a student and family assistance program that has become a national model of effectiveness. Total Community Solution teams of teachers, administrators, and support staff come together at each of the district's buildings to develop a plan whenever a student demonstrates a need for intervention.

An important part of the TCS is the Garfield Heights Youth, Family & Teen Services (GYFTS) program that provides social workers in each of the district's buildings. The Garfield Heights Alternative Juvenile Program, a Community Diversion program, is a unique collaboration between the Cuyahoga County Court of Common Pleas, the Juvenile Court and the community which provides magistrates to hear student cases referred by the school or the community. The program utilizes the "sternness of the bench" and the "kindness of a guidance counselor approach" in dealing with students violating rules, regulations, and the district's Code of Conduct. The Total Community Solution (TCS) program is a comprehensive approach to be sure no student falls through the cracks. Parents are encouraged to take advantage of the broad range of services designed by the district to assist them with the many challenges of raising a family today.

In addition to the Total Community Solution, the district boosts a special education program that meets the need of every child, including gifted children, in the most appropriate setting. Terrence Deal (2001), co-author of the best-selling book, *Leading With Soul* visited the district and stated "Superintendent Victor is a man with heart that demonstrates leading with soul."

The Future

In the summer of 2001, the superintendent and the Mayor of this community took the next step and invited 110 community leaders to come together for a leadership conference. Prior to the conference, each invitee was provided a copy of Warren Blank's (2001) latest book, *The 108 Skills of Natural Born Leaders*. At the conference, Dr. Blank presented a workshop on leadership providing information on the skills necessary for natural born leaders. From this conference, these questions emerged:

In the Year 2050...

1. What does Garfield Heights look like? What is special and unique about it? What role does education play? How does the city contribute to a positive lifestyle?

2. How do you contribute to the vision? What exactly do you do?

3. How did the school system and/or city leadership help you do these things?

Responses from those who attended the leadership conference have provided the basis for six objectives:

1. Visionary Leadership
2. Excellent Schools
3. All-Inclusive Recreation
4. Attractive Retail
5. Outstanding Cooperation
6. Quality Housing

In October of 2003, over 200 community leaders were invited to attend a 2nd leadership conference to further Leadership Garfield Heights.

Also supporting these objectives is information from the Imagine Garfield Heights program. Imagine Garfield Heights is a unique program involving students from Garfield Heights High School who have been trained utilizing the skills of "Appreciative Inquiry." This information, together with the information from the leadership conference, now provides the learning community, superintendent, and mayor objectives on which to build the future of this community. The most challenging objective for this district continues to be "meeting the needs of the heart" by improving the culture within each classroom recognizing that parent involvement make a huge difference. Building positive relationship between parents, teachers and students is paramount to the success of all children. At the start of 2003-2004 they implemented a new contract for each parent called: Priority One: Parent Contract for Success, asking each principal, teacher and parent in the district to make a commitment to be involved with child for the entire school year. The contract asks each parent to select from a list of activities to become more involved in their child's educational plan. Also to address the requirements of the *No Child Left Behind Act,* the district began the 2003-2004 school year with the theme "Changing for the Future." A new plan to improve student instruction and performance on proficiency tests titled *Priority One: The Cycle of Success* was implemented under the leadership of an Instructional Focus Team (IFT). This highly motivated team of school leaders includes principals and teachers. *Priority One: The Cycle of Success* identifies that student improvement and improved instruction begins with the teacher and support from competent instruction leaders.

The Garfield Heights City Schools was awarded a three year $3.9 million dollar grant by the United States Department of Education to continue the district's efforts to "meet the needs of the heart." The grant will provide support for elementary guidance counselors, school social workers, and school psychologists to assist families to deal with the social ills facing communities today. Creating an invitational environment includes programs that emphasize the importance of positive and healthy relationships between students and teachers.

The learning community of Garfield Heights truly is inviting. The community, its schools and its leaders are shining examples of invitational community entrepreneurship that continually look for ways to create an invitational environment that includes programs that emphasize the importance of positive and healthy relationships between parents, teachers and students.

References

Blank, W. (2001). *The 108 skills of natural born leaders*. New York: AMACOM.

Bolman, L.G. & Deal T.E. (2001) *Leading with soul: an uncommon journey of spirit*. San Franciso: Jossey-Bass.

Chapter 7

Getting There:
Creating Inviting Climates

Tommie Radd

How do we create classrooms and schools that support students in becoming their best? What needs to happen so students learn? How do students learn ways to develop and contribute their unique gifts?

Research (Purkey & Novak, 1996; Purkey, 2000) and experience shows the essential role and impact of inviting climates and invitational education, yet how often do the best of intentions get sidetracked with unsuccessful results. What can be done to create and maintain the invitational stance plus support on-going growth? How do we support our teachers, counselors, administrators, and all those in the school community so that growth can occur?

To reach the goals of invitational education these questions need to be answered. Invitational education is based in self-concept theory and the perceptional psychology tradition, yet many of the plans for school improvement and creating inviting schools and classroom experiences do not consider the ways these elements develop. Usually, the personal, emotional, social, and behavioral skills that are needed for a positive self-concept and self-perception to develop are not included in the plan. Without them it is difficult to get achievement desired and inviting climate maintained. It is difficult to help students develop their spirit, purpose, and potential (Radd, 2003).

Developing a Frame of Reference and a Different Result

Self-concept and self-perception evolve through a process of learning about self and others through experiences and relationships with people and information. The processes and experiences needed to create an inviting climate can become a frame of reference that supports students' success in all areas. Regardless of students' backgrounds, experiences and skills learned in school can provide students with the tools they need to make helpful life choices for their future (Novak & Purkey, 2001).

This chapter outlines a plan that is clear and concise, conscious, and intentional regarding ways to develop this frame of reference based in self-concept and the perceptual psychology tradition. We know we need a different approach if we want to reach a different result from those we are getting. This chapter discusses the implementation of a research and results-based guidance systems model process to create and maintain an inviting school climate. Our discussion begins by assessing the difference between a traditional classroom and the real classroom (Radd, 2003).

The Heart of the Classroom and School

Figure 1

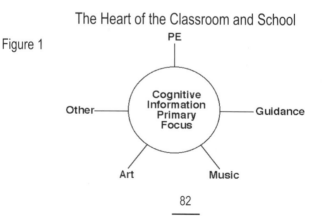

Figure 2

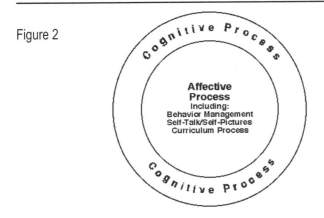

Cognitive Process

Affective Process
Including:
Behavior Management
Self-Talk/Self-Pictures
Curriculum Process

Cognitive Process

The Traditional Classroom

Traditional classrooms include a strong academic tradition that at one time may have worked effectively for student learning. Traditional classrooms and guidance programs place guidance outside of the classroom. The traditional classroom perceives guidance as an "extra service" provided for certain students with problems or needs. Guidance is not officially an integral part of what goes on in the classroom. When there is a concern of funding cuts within a school, the guidance program is seen as a possible "cut" because of its "outside the traditional classroom" position.

In a traditional classroom skills that require learning to occur don't officially include the guidance process skills of effective communication, cooperation, collaboration, and responsible interactions with self and others. The primary subjects of language arts, mathematics, science, and social studies are viewed as separate from guidance process skills. There's no defined affective component or guidance system. Usually students are not viewed in a holistic manner and cognitive subject matter "minutes" drive the curriculum. The focus of this classroom is subject centered and not student centered.

We know that personal, social, emotional, and behavioral factors impact the traditional classroom, even though they are not identified or addressed. We know that those factors occur constantly and impact whether a climate is inviting and if students can succeed. The real classroom identifies all factors that are needed for an inviting climate and puts those processes in place for success. Developmental guidance systems are the heart of real classrooms (Radd, 2003, 2000 & 1996 a&b).

The Real Classroom

The real classroom recognizes the truth that education is a human experiential process that is done through various interactions "with" students. Students are viewed holistically and the learning environment is centered upon the developmental learning needs of the student and a healthy, balanced, classroom climate. Guidance process skills of effective communication, cooperation, collaboration, and responsible interactions with self and others are central skills to the learning process in all curriculum areas. Life-long learning is viewed as a process that is addressed in all student domains. Behavior and the self-talk/self-pictures process are viewed as a part of learning and central to life-long learning in all areas.

A comprehensive, developmental guidance system is at the heart of the real classroom. The developmental guidance system includes specific ingredients that create an intentional process needed for the inviting environment to evolve. The components of the system develop a central core from which all learning interactions generate. This systems model and systemic process include:

◆ cooperative learning

◆ facilitative processes

◆ peer listening

◆ a solid self-concept approach

◆ the core skills needed for personal, social, emotional, and behavioral skills to develop

◆ the core for effective behavior management where all behavior is a part of learning

◆ the core for effective self-talk and self-pictures

◆ the process to create an inviting environment with self and others in the classroom and school

Academic curriculum builds on this process. The only constant in a classroom is the personal, emotional, social, and behavioral interaction that affects everything. No matter what is being taught, students' self-awareness, personal skills, and perceptions will influence and often determine results. No matter what is being taught, emotions are always happening and will influence and often determine results. No matter what is being taught, social interactions and perceptions influence and often determine results. No matter what is being taught, behavior is always happening and influences learning for all students.

The developmental guidance system is for all students. The system includes a positive behavior management plan, a positive self-talk/self-pictures plan, a student skill and curriculum plan, a staff skill development plan, a family support and development plan, and an accountability process. The developmental guidance system is the foundation of the guidance and counseling program and the central core and heart of the classroom. The next section provides an overview of the guidance systems model and components (Radd, 2003, 2000, 1996a, & 1996b).

The Developmental Guidance
System Model Overview

Real classrooms are designed proactively and include a developmental guidance system as a foundation. This requires that traditional guidance curriculum have a broader comprehensive, developmental, competency-based focus. The real classroom applies guidance concepts and personal, social, emotional, and behavioral skills developed through the guidance activities and experiences in the day-to-day happenings at school. For example, during a math class, students are able to state their strengths and challenges about their assignment, communicate their feelings, relate to other students and the teacher in the class, and show appropriate behavior to support their learning. Also, the self-concept series and weave is integrated throughout the developmental guidance system as a process for developing positive self-perception and integrating positive self-concept into life skills.

The Self-Concept Series and Weave

The foundation of each component of the guidance system is the self-concept series and weave. It is important to introduce and integrate the self-concept series and weave into the classroom and school building. The self-concept series, consisting of three steps, is taught and integrated for *all* students.

This self-concept series process is used to teach people, especially students, how to separate the truth of their worth from their behavior while holding them accountable for their choices. The three steps of the self-concept series are:

1. Truth, Unconditional Acceptance: People are special and valuable because they are unique and different from each other.

2. Behavior: Because people are special and unique, they have a responsibility to help and not hurt themselves or others. People show they are remembering that they are important by the way they choose to act. If people choose to hurt themselves or others, they are forgetting that they are special and valuable. Likewise, if people choose to help themselves or others, they are remembering that they are special. When people help themselves, they are also helping other people through demonstration and positive results.

3. Accountability: People are responsible to "watch" their actions to determine if they are remembering the *truth* that they are special. People are "with" themselves at all times and are accountable to remember to treat themselves *and others* as important people.

After the self-concept series is introduced to students, the three steps are elicited from students to determine their level of understanding. The greater the number of adults and students who use, understand, and believe this self-concept process, the greater the opportunities for students to relate the information and experience into their knowledge base and life-skill understanding of self-concept.

The self-concept series is the base on the self-concept series weave. The concepts are taught, reviewed, connected and woven throughout each day-to-day experience that relates to the life experiences of students. The self-concept series and weave are the base of the guidance system and components and build up students by separating student worth from their behavior choices (Radd, 1996a, 1996b, 2000a, & 2000b).

A Developmental Guidance System—The Foundation

Figure 3

Figure 4

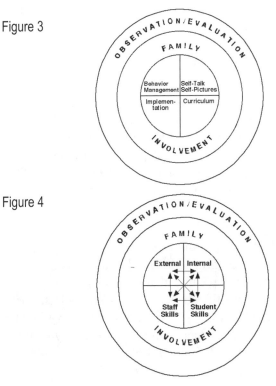

The Foundation System (Radd, 1996a, 1996b, & 2000a) includes six interactive components: behavior management, self-talk/self-pictures, student, staff, and family development and skills, and observation/evaluation. The Foundation System is a system because it incorporates an interactive plan for behavior, self-talk/self-pictures, and curriculum. Consistent implementation of all three—behavior, self-talk/self-pictures, and curriculum—create the foundation and environment for positive results. Staff skill development, family support and development, and observation/evaluation also are components of the System.

Self-concept is developed through day to day interactions with students. It is important that all interactions with students support a healthy self-concept. This can be accomplished though implementation of the self-concept series/weave process throughout each component of the guidance foundation system. A brief explanation of each component and references follows:

Behavior Management Component

The Behavior Management Component allows behavior to become a part of the learning process for both students and staff. This component provides the framework for healthy interactions in which behavioral challenges become opportunities for greater understanding and growth (Child Development Project, 1996; Dreikurs, Grunwald & Pepper, 1998; Emmet, et al., 1996; Glasser, 1998; Radd & Ficenec, 1996; Radd, 1996a, 1996b, 1998 & 2000a).

Self-Talk/Self-Pictures Component

Self-Talk/Self-Pictures is the process that allows "what we say and believe" to be congruent with "what we think and feel." The internal thoughts and pictures that students hold need to be supportive of the positive life goals of the student. Selected self-talk/self-pictures can be used to support the positive behavior plan and other guidance system components (Manning & Payne, 1995) (Purkey, 2000; Seligman, 1995; Radd, 1996a, 1996b, & 2000a).

Curriculum Component

As the behavior and the self-talk/self-pictures plans begins and continue to be implemented the environment and the internal base is established for the system activity process to be successful. This activity process implemented simultaneously with the other components provides the information and experiences for the development of a student skill base. These skills are in the strands of Self, Other Awareness, Self-Control, Decision Making/Problem Solving, Group Cooperation, and Career. The Children's Affect Needs Assessment (CANA) is used to determine the students' perception of their skill needs and for students' ownership of their skill-building process. Also, strand competencies are identified and prioritized. The combination of the CANA results and the development skill priorities determine the curriculum focus for each classroom of students (Johnson & Johnson, 1999) (Purkey, 1970; Radd & Brightman, 1996; Radd, 1996a, 1996b, & 2000a).

Staff Development Component

This component supports the development of skills and approaches that are most effective for professionals and their students. In staff development sessions and in classroom modeling, it is important to demonstrate and create experiences that support a personal and professional growth plan for staff. Slowly, staff members learn guidance skills and apply and relate those skills into the guidance system components and the academic learning processes. The staff learns personal, social, emotional, and behavioral skills and processes as they participate with the designated guidance professional and follow-up with students. There is a reciprocal relationship between what we learn and what we teach. Staff involvement in the system process becomes a support for the staff, while helping students learn to develop in all domains. The Invitational Teaching Survey—Primary & Intermediate (ITS-P&I) is used to determine the students' perception of their teacher's personally and professionally inviting practices. The combination of the ITS-P&I results and skill priorities from staff needs assessments and designated competencies determine the staff development focus (Purkey & Novak, 1996; Radd, 1994,1996a, 1996b, 1996c, & 2000a).

Family Involvement Component

The Family Component has two primary emphases: (1) Family feedback regarding application of student skills at home; and (2) Family support and education. The use of the information provided in the other components can be used in family education (Radd, 1996a, 1996b, & 2000a).

System Observation/Evaluation

The comprehensive Observation/Evaluation process for the system includes balanced and planned qualitative and quantitative approaches. An example of a plan that can be used as a basis for a progress report is:

◆ Use the pre and post CANA results for quantitative results in student perception of their change in their Self, Other Awareness, Self-Control, Decision Making/Problem Solving, and Group Cooperation skills.

◆ Use the pre and post ITS-P&I results for the quantitative results in students perception of the change they observe in their teacher's personally and professionally inviting practices.

◆ Use qualitative feedback based on the prioritized competencies in each component and the total system.

The focus is positive observation not deficits. The positive focus on results gives an opportunity to report and celebrate gains while making adjustments and additions for the 3-5 year guidance system implementation. Prioritized established goals, competencies and results are the basis for the observation/evaluation process. Information feedback from students, staff and families needs to be included (Radd, 1988, 1996a, 1996b, & 2000a).

The Guidance System Organization Plan

The guidance system needs to be organized with a 3 to 5 year plan that supports learning and gradual change. Each component is implemented slowly and simultaneously over this 3-5 year time period with each system component being implemented in part annually. This process supports the guidance system prioritized goals, competencies, and results so they can be realized for students, staff, and families. The guidance and counseling administrator, the director of curriculum, or a similar designee would coordinate the system organization, in most cases. Input from an advisory committee that is representative of the school and community populations can be helpful.

The building counselor or designated professional in most cases would coordinate the system at the building level. An organizational team needs to be identified and the process for the system implementation needs to be decided and communicated within the school district. Consistent organization within the buildings of the district is recommended due to the curricular and comprehensive nature of the guidance system and the increased transient nature of student populations.

Counselor-teacher teams are organized at the beginning of the school year and are recommended for maximum results. If a school does not have a counselor, a professional trained in facilitation and developmental guidance and counseling can be used to work as a team member with the teacher (Radd, 1994, 1998, 1996a, 1996b, & 2000a).

Classroom Life Labs

The process of implementing a developmental guidance system creates a classroom and school that is a "life lab" of essential student experiences needed for life-long learning. Students learn personal, social, emotional, and behavioral skills through guidance curriculum. They practice and apply those skills as behavior challenges occur and make adjustments. Students assess their self-talk and self-pictures and make adjustments that support helpful behaviors and learning. Students and staff have the skills for effective communication that enhance learning and their relationships. The self-concept series and weave is included throughout the process so students realize their positive self-concept.

Students become empowered and learn ways to respond and not react in life so they can develop their spirit, purpose and potential.

The Place of the Foundation System in the Guidance & Counseling Program

Figure 5

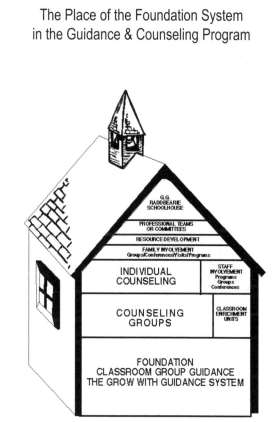

Figure 6

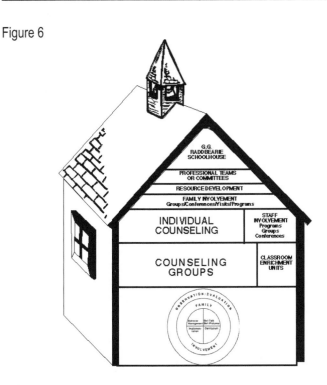

An interactive, systematic counseling program is built upon the developmental foundation system. All program components are consistently represented throughout the elementary through high school program. Developmentally appropriate content and variations on the amount of designated time per component is the primary differentiation among counseling levels. All program components, elementary through high school, require the framework of goals, competencies, and results in order to maintain a results-based counseling program. Components of the guidance and counseling program and suggestions for the counselor's program time allocations at the elementary (E), Middle School (MS), and High School (HS) levels are:

◆ The Foundation: A Developmental Guidance System—

93

40% of the counselor's time allocation, Elementary School (E); 30% to 35% of the counselor's time allocation, Middle School (MS); and 25% to 30% of the counselor's time allocation, High School (HS)

◆ Counseling Groups: 30% of the counselor's time allocation (E); 30% to 35% of the counselor's time allocation (MS & HS)

◆ Individual Counseling: 10% of a counselor's time allocation. (E, MS, & HS)

The remaining 20% of the counselor's time include items 4-8:

◆ Classroom Enrichment Units

◆ Staff Involvement—Programs/Groups/Conferences

◆ Family Involvement Programs/Groups/Conferences

◆ Resource Development

◆ Professional Teams/Committees

Consultation, cooperation, communication, coordination, collaboration, and facilitation are important within each component of the foundation system and program in working with students, staff, families, and the community.

Observation/Evaluation is needed to demonstrate accountability and maintain a results-based guidance system and program focused on results. The positive focus on results gives an opportunity to report and celebrate gains in all program areas while making adjustments and additions for the 3-5 year implementation process. Goals, competencies, and results are integral within each system and program component. This observation/evaluation process needs to be structured as an on-going and annual component of the guidance system and program (Radd, 1996a&b & 2000a).

Programs need to be designed proactively for success and demonstrate student results and program accountability. This requires that guidance and counseling programs begin to have a broader comprehensive, developmental, competency-based focus. Expand-

ing the way we view guidance and counseling from a service or program into a system is the key. The guidance program components such as the classroom group guidance system foundation, small group counseling, and individual counseling are systematically interrelated and applied in the guidance and counseling program. For example, the skills and experiences students and staff learn in the developmental guidance system affect the ways students and staff interact and helps them develop a positive relationship. Students who would benefit from a small counseling group need to apply skills and experiences from the foundation in the group. Students who would benefit from additional individual counseling need to apply the skills and experiences from the classroom experience to their challenge. Student success throughout the developmental guidance and counseling program comes through applying and practicing skills learned in the foundation (Radd, 1996a & 2000a).

A systems approach is interactive, interrelated, interconnected, and congruent and is the basis for a successful guidance and counseling program. An interactive system identifies those program components that affect each other. For example, the success of the guidance curriculum is based on congruent daily interactions of adults with students so what is taught is modeled and experienced by students. An interrelated system identifies those daily happenings that include guidance and counseling skills and concepts such as higher ordered thinking and the needed guidance decision making and communication skills. An interconnected system identifies how everything in the guidance program connects with the school program and learning process such as students communicating concerns and feelings about achievement and teaching adjustments being made to meet student needs. A congruent system identifies those programs, policies, and daily processes in the school that fit with the concepts and skills developed through the guidance program such as congruence between the school student conduct plan and the school district policy.

A guidance systems approach is central to the daily success of the educational process for all students and essential for the development of positive self-concept and self-perception. Also, a systems approach identifies those components of the educational process that can sabotage counseling and other program results (Radd, 1996a & 2000a).

Invitational Education Focuses on the Heart of Education

Invitational education focuses on the heart of education. The important role of an inviting classroom climate provides a rich environment for both personal and professional messages to be given and received. Invitational education's balanced approach to the teaching and learning process is essential if we are to invite students to become self-actualized, fulfilled human beings in all areas including academic. By implementing a developmental guidance system and counseling program, we can reach the goals of invitational education, have a conscious and intentional plan and process to create, support, and maintain an inviting school.

In addition to the positive impact of creating an inviting climate in each classroom, there is the additional impact of enhanced staff skill development and support on expanding the inviting climate throughout each school in a school district. Staff programs and communication about invitational education are also organized and implemented. Personal and professional growth plans are important for all staff members. This supports an ongoing growth process, which injects energy, enthusiasm, and positive attitudes into the day-to-day experiences with students. Professional teams and committees may develop a strategic "invitational" plan to communicate the desired staff growth process.

The following are benefits and results of having a guidance system at the heart of the classroom, school program and school design. These benefits create and maintain an inviting environment:

◆ there is a plan for change that is an integral part of the day-to-day operation of the school

◆ there is a conscious plan to support the self-concept development of all within the school

◆ the perception of students, staff and families is communicated and modified when it is destructive

◆ personal, social, emotional and behavioral skills are taught

◆ students provide ongoing feedback to educators as to their day-to-day experience in school

◆ there is an intentional process for consciously creating an inviting environment for all students

◆ there is congruence between the behavior management approaches, student self-talk/ self-pictures, student skills, and staff skills

◆ each classroom is seen as a "life lab" where students develop a frame of reference for success in all areas of life

◆ there is an intentional process for students to develop personally, socially, emotionally, behaviorally, and intellectually (Radd, 2003).

Conclusion

This chapter provides information needed for the answers to our beginning questions. The personal, emotional, behavioral, and social skills needed in life are learned through the system process. Classroom "life labs" create the experiences students need for a positive frame of reference. As they evolve throughout life, students have practice and skills to use higher ordered thinking to handle change. Students learn information about self, others and applications for life success that integrate academics and allow for them to apply that knowledge as they grow and life requirements change. The plan outlined is a process that is conscious, intentional, and multi-dimensional and can result in an inviting environment and climate. Positive self-concept and self-perception are integrated within the process and can help students develop their spirit, purpose, and potential (Radd, 2003).

References

Child Development Project (1996). *Ways we want our class to be: Class meetings that build commitment to kindness and learning.* Oakland, CA: Developmental Studies Center.

Dreikurs, R., Grunwald, B., & Pepper, F. (1998). *Maintaining sanity in the classroom: classroom management techniques.* (2nd ed.) Washington, DC: Accelerated Development; Bristol PA: Distribution Office, Taylor & Francis.

Emmet, J., Monsour,S., Lundeberg,M., Russo,T., Secrist, K., Lindquist,N., Moriarity, S., & Uhren,P. (1996). Open classroom meetings: Promoting peaceful schools. *Elementary School Guidance & Counseling Journal 31,* 3-10.

Fidler, J. (1999). Discussion concerning school-based research. Westside Community Schools, Omaha, NE.

Glasser, W. (1998). *Choice theory in the classroom.* New York: Harper Perennial.

Johnson, D. W., & Johnson, R. (1999). (5th ed.). *Learning together and alone: Cooperative, competitive, and individualistic learning.* Boston, MA: Allyn and Bacon

Manning, Brenda H. & Payne, Beverly D. (1995). *Self-talk for teachers and students.* Needham Heights, MA: Allyn & Bacon.

Novak, J. M. & Purkey, W.W. (2001). *Invitational education.* Fastback 488. Bloomington, IN: Phi Delta Kappa Educational Foundation.

Purkey, W.W. (1970). *Self-concept and school achievement.* Englewood Cliffs, NJ: Prentice Hall.

Purkey, W.W. & Cage, B.N. (1973). The Florida key: A scale to infer learner self-concept. *Educational Psychological Measurement, 33,* 979-984.

Purkey, W.W., & Novak, J. M.(1996). *Inviting school success* (Third Edition). Belmont, CA: Wadsworth Publishing.

Purkey, W.W. (2000). *What students say to themselves, internal dialogue and school success.* Thousand Oaks, CA: Corwin Press.

Radd, T. R. (1988). *The effects of grow with guidance on self-concept as learner and teacher self-concept.* Doctoral dissertation, The University of Akron. Dissertation Abstracts International.

Radd, T.R. (1996a). *The grow with guidance system manual.* (2nd ed.). Canton,OH: Grow With Guidance.

Radd, T. R. (1996b). *The grow with guidance system levels 1-9.* (2nd ed.). Canton, OH: Grow With Guidance.

Radd, T. R. (1996c). *The invitational teaching survey-primary & intermediate.* Second Edition. Canton, OH: Grow With Guidance

Radd, T. R. (1994). Creating the inviting classroom through the use of a competency-based guidance system. *Journal of Invitational Theory and Practice, 3*(2), 95-107.

Radd, T. R. & Ficenec, Anne. (1996). Creating a healthy classroom climate while facilitating behavior change: A self-concept approach. Ideas exchange. *Elementary School Guidance and Counseling Journal.* December, *31*(2), 153-158.

Radd, T. R. (1998). Developing an inviting classroom climate through a comprehensive behavior management plan. *The Journal of Invitational Theory and Practice, 5*(1), 19-30.

Radd, T. R. (1998). Designing an outcome based school counseling system and program. *School Counseling: New Perspectives & Practices.* Greensboro, NC: ERIC CASS, 93-97.

Radd, T. R. (2000a). *Getting from here to there . . . Education for the new millennium.* Omaha, NE: Grow With Guidance.

Radd, T. R. (2000b). Integrating self-concept into life skills. In C. L. Thompson & L. Rudolph, *Counseling Children* (5th ed), 152-155. Belmont, CA: Brooks/Cole.

Radd, T. R. (2003). *Teaching and counseling for today's world.* Omaha, NE: Grow With Guidance.

Radd, T.R. & Brightman, B. (1996). *The children's affect needs assessment.* (2nd ed). Canton, OH: Grow With Guidance.

Seligman, M. (1995). *The optimistic child.* New York: Houghton Mifflin.

Chapter 8

A Guide to Inviting
On-Line Education:
Welcome to the On-Line
World of Education

Tony DiPetta, John Novak, and Zopito Marini

The landscape of contemporary education presents a frenetic
world of instantaneous communication. What we seem to have is
a well-wired and, ironically, an increasingly wireless environment
where technophiles and technophobes wait to see where this focus
on all things technological is leading education. The technophiles
are those educators who are quite sophisticated in an ever-expanding array of information and communication technology (ICT).
Technophiles generally believe that technology will save education
from its ills and lead to a brave new wireless world of teaching and
learning. Technophobes, on the other hand, are fearful at "brave new
technological worlds" and feel overwhelmed. These technological
"have-nots" are dubious about the cost, complexity, over-reliance,
and ever increasing demands for speed and power that information
and communication technologies in education demand. To these
people these technologies are insidious gadgetry, taking over their
professional lives and prying into their private lives as well. Some
technophobes nostalgically yearn for the "Good Old Days," the
illusionary time when the human touch was thought to be ever-pres-

ent and machines knew their place and kept a respectful distance. Others fear the intrusive and arcane nature of what they perceive as the unreal world of "techies" and "cyberspace."

The majority of educators in the increasingly technological landscape of education are neither fanatical technophiles nor exasperated technophobes. The majority are simply educators and administrators prudently asking, "what's information and communication technology all about and what can it do for education?" To the delight of the technophiles, and the dismay of the technophobes, information and communication technology appears to be gaining in both popularity and application. A report by the U.S. census bureau indicates that at the start of the new millennium 51% of U.S households have computers and Internet access (U.S. Census Report, 2001). At the same time schools in the United States have spent over 8 billion dollars on desktop computers, software, and infrastructure for Internet access (Smerdon & Cronen, 2000). Furthermore, more than 50% of U.S. high schools currently offer online courses to their students (CyberAtlas, Feb.19, 2002).

The rapid acceptance and spread of on-line education, loosely defined as the use of information and communication technologies to deliver, support, or supplement classroom instruction, holds enormous implications for schools, educators, and society. The use of such technology in education needs to be examined prudently by everyone, including those repelled by, and those smitten by, ICT's power and potential. For technophobes, this means overcoming some anxieties and fears that are roadblocks to dealing with on-line education's possibilities. For technophiles, this means understanding the anxieties and concerns of those that are less than experts in technological usage and recognising the possible problems that unbridled enthusiasm for technological solutions to educational challenges might obscure. For those who are neither technophile nor technophobe, this means being open to discussion about ICT in teaching and learning and being willing to critically assess what on-line education can and cannot do. For all groups, this means examining the intended and unintended consequences of on-line education. Technophobes, technophiles, and the rest will all benefit from a prudent approach to on-line education, whether it is at a distance or adapted for use in a traditional classroom, that attempts to be intentional, informed, inviting, integrated, and imaginative.

Invitational education (Purkey & Novak, 1996; Novak & Purkey, 2001; DiPetta, Novak & Marini, 2002) provides a theory of practice that can be of assistance to educators who seek to work from a democratically-oriented, person-centered perspective in developing on-line educational environments. In North American schools education is viewed as a fundamental component of democratic society. From an invitational perspective the public practice of education is seen as an imaginative act of hope that involves a commitment to the development of individual potential and social practices that enable all involved to savour, understand, and better their personal and social experiences (Novak, 2002). On-line educational possibilities need to be grounded in such hope and imaginative acts if they are to be ethical endeavours for educational growth and development. The educational hope emphasized here is not merely that students and teachers will become competent in dealing with the on-line world, but that they, and everyone involved in the educative process, will critically examine the underlying assumptions and consequences of on-line education.

A prudent perspective on technology is called for because a commitment to technology in education is not value-neutral. Such a commitment involves an investment of time, effort, money, and the re-allocation of other scarce resources into the development of a technologically-mediated education system that is based on instantaneous communication and information gratification that, at present, privileges certain technological, economic, social, and personal interests.

On-line education, therefore, has to go beyond merely technical and psychological rationales to justify its expanding adoption by, and influence in, the education community. The larger social implications of on-line education also need to be considered. The technologically prudent approach to on-line teaching and learning alerts everyone to be mindful of issues and concerns that might be ignored by the heartiest technophiles and the staunchest technophobes. A prudent and inviting approach to online teaching and learning moves beyond the narrow confines of technical or practical effectiveness into the heart of democratic educational development for schools where information and communication technology is used to develop virtual environments that invite human growth and development through the support or delivery of instruction.

The Mythology of On-line Education

A great deal of current practice with regard to technology in education is based on an overarching mythology that maintains that "Technology is the Answer!" This myth has become the battle cry implicit in many approaches to on-line education. It assumes, however, that there is common agreement on the what, how, and why of technology's use in education. When it comes to technology in education, it is clear that, one size does not fit all. If as the mythology suggests "technology is the answer" it is incumbent on all prudent educators to ask, "Are we posing the right pedagogical questions?"

The pedagogical effectiveness of on-line education depends on an inter-related number of factors including, but not limited to, the type of course, the teacher, the level of instruction, and the student. It may well be that not every student will benefit from on-line education, but there is little doubt that all students benefit from interacting with a caring and supportive teacher. On-line education will succeed as an educative environment to the extent that teachers and school administrators are able to provide a democratic on-line structure that preserves dignity and encourages communication. Alternatively, if teachers use technology to overload students with information then on-line environments will freeze students in their tracks, like deer caught in the headlights of speeding cars.

There is still much research and reflection needed to determine what on-line education should, can, or cannot do. The following myths about on-line education are presented for prudent consideration and discussion by all groups investigating the use of technology for teaching and learning.

1. The Myth of Easy Proof and Evaluation

Many technophiles suggest that the benefits of technology's use in education are both obvious and easily evaluated. However, much of the evidence provided for such claims is anecdotal and subject to a variety of interpretations. Whether student learning is improved or enhanced through the use of information and communication technology may someday be empirically determined but until then we should resist simplistic comparisons of on-line education to traditional instruction. Erhmann (1999) notes that learning is not so well-structured or consistently defined to enable researchers to compare a technology or innovation against a "traditional" process without going into great detail about what that process is. Erhmann (1999) reminds us that defining what is meant by traditional in terms of materials, methods, and motives limits research to very small and time dependent samples. This does not mean that we should not evaluate, but rather that determining with any empirical certainty how effective on-line education is will take considerable time, effort, and long-term testing.

2. The Myth of Revolutionary Education

Technology may well have the potential to revolutionize education, but simply wiring schools and providing teachers and students with computers and Internet access will never have the impact of a "shot heard round the world." The nexus of educational software and school programming often tends to create a rigidity of structure and use that cannot address the increasingly varied needs that students bring to school. Education is an important and complex human undertaking that cannot be delegated to an electronic script. On-line technology will revolutionise teaching only to the degree that it can be used as a tool for communicating and deepening human experience. Information and communication technology can provide greater numbers of students with access to information that they might not have been able to access before, but this is not the same as students developing an understanding of important concepts and the interplay of ideas. Perkins (1992) notes that understanding is a consequence of thinking and not merely receiving information. Confusion between "informing" and "educating" abound, requiring the technologically prudent to distinguish between having access to the wealth of information that technology can provide and inviting students to reach new depths of understanding and personal growth that develop through face-to-face interaction. Thus there is little agreement on what educational roles and purposes information and communication technologies should serve in the classroom. Every teacher, administrator, student, and parent may have a different view on what is necessary, possible, or even feasible with on-line technology and much more experimentation and reflection needs to be done before we can say with any degree of certainty what will work and what will not in on-line education practice.

3. The Myth that More is Better, Faster, and Cheaper

Today most schools have computers, Internet access, and a variety of software programs for teaching and learning. And yet all this technology alone cannot significantly change teaching practice or academic outcomes for the majority of students (Schacter & Fagnano, 1999). Technology, in and of itself, does not create positive change in schools or practice. There is ample evidence, however, that caring and dedicated teachers can and do make a positive difference in schools and in students lives. Technology may make a difference in student academic success in specific subject or skills areas, but only if teachers and programs explicitly target the use of technology to reach these educational goals. Learning about technology is not the same as learning to teach with technology. The road to better schools may be paved with technology, but it will be planned and built by teachers.

Another component of the myth of more technology is better suggests that having more technology will save teachers and students time and effort. However, for many teachers and students learning to work with on-line technology is time consuming, difficult, and inconvenient. Consider a teacher who wants to use a simulation in a high school history course. The teacher must research and find a suitable software simulation that is licensed by the school and that will run on the machines available in the school lab. Next the teacher must learn to use the simulation and experiment with how it might be used in class. Once the lesson is planned, lab schedules, teaching students to work with the simulation, and unforeseen technical problems may limit the amount of in-class time that can be allotted for the lesson. Some teachers clearly view preparing a technologically supported lesson as a much greater demand on their time and energy than preparing a classroom activity without technology. The extra effort and planning involved in technologically-mediated lessons may also promote anxieties about technology and about risking scarce lesson time that some teachers view as less than dependable supplements to more traditional classroom methods (Di Petta, Novak, & Marini, 2001).

The final aspect of this myth suggests that on-line technologies reduce the need for teachers and classrooms, and ultimately save schools money. However, the full costs of information and communication technology in schools are not easily measured or monitored. Infrastructure, maintenance, and upgrading costs are on-going and not a one-time expense for schools. Moreover, development expenses and reasonable estimates for teacher time, training, and support staff expenditures are often omitted from the cost estimates for on-line technology. Ultimately, even if on-line technology enables schools to reduce the number of teachers, and the number of classrooms or labs, or to increase class size, such cost benefits may be offset by the need for hardware and infrastructure upgrades, and more people in technical support roles. More technology does not reduce the need for teachers, rather it increases the need for continuous teacher training to develop and practice the skills needed to work with technology.

4. The Myth of Cyber-Equality and Empowerment

The desire to bridge what has been called the "cyber divide" that separates the "have" and the "have-not" schools in terms of on-line technology is laudable. However, providing information and communication technology to all schools does little to address the other social, political, and economic conditions that contribute to the disparities that separate "have" and "have-not" schools and students in North America. Many schools with technology often lack the means and funding for teacher technology training and support. Teacher, student, and parental attitudes towards student success and ability may also differ and shape how technology is used in the classroom. Students in economically disadvantaged areas and schools are much more likely to use computers for drill-and-practice and supplementary learning tasks. Schools in more prosperous areas are more likely to use computer technology in project-based applications that are tied to problem-solving or inquiry and collaborative learning activities where the student is working with the on-line technology to achieve an educational goal and not as a supplementary activity to learning.

Information and communication technologies, it is often claimed by technology manufacturers and technophiles, have the capability of empowering educators and learners to achieve higher levels of personal fulfilment and educational creativity. However the many innovative and successful on-line education programs and courses that exist are not the result of the technology alone but rather these exemplary programs are the result of the commitment, expertise, and resourcefulness of individual teachers who have dedicated their time and skills to developing and sustaining person-centered programs for working with technology in education. These programs and courses rise and fall with the willingness of dedicated teachers to contribute their time and energy to maintaining and using technology in creative ways. For some teachers, working with technology is a leap of faith that hones their professional skills in the classroom and reinforces their personal beliefs in the efficacy of on-line education. For others, who may lack adequate support, training, or a technological inclination, technology demands a personal discipline and commitment that is neither liberating nor empowering. Invitational theory suggests that teaching is not a "technology" and teachers are not "technicians" and on-line education is simply another environment in which the complex and important human interaction of teaching takes place.

5. The Myth of On-line Gold

The final myth about on-line education is that the digital world is a gold mine of information just waiting to be tapped by students and teachers to meet their pedagogical and personal goals. According to current research, the Internet contains an estimated four billion pages of information, and this is increasing at the rate of 100% a year (Lyman & Varia, 2000). Such a vast amount of information for research purposes is certainly a gold mine for education, or so it would seem at first glance. However, as Shakespeare reminds us, "all that glitters is not gold." There are currently few ways for most users of online resources to verify the accuracy of information available in cyberspace and much of the available information is general in nature and not always presented in a clearly organised or accessible manner. According to an article in the Toronto Star, it has been estimated that the percentage of information on the Internet that is useful to any particular person is in the area of 0.01 percent and dropping (July 20, 2000). There are certainly nuggets of gold in the on-line mine for teachers and students to find, but more often than not, such nuggets are buried under mountains of irrelevant, inappropriate, or downright dangerous information that prudent educators must sift, refine, and examine critically.

Good teachers have always mentored, coached, facilitated, and encouraged their students by engaging them in active learning. Having an inviting and prudent frame of reference is a way to become more intentional, integrated, and imaginative in the thoughtful practice of on-line education, for it is a constant reminder of what is truly important in education-an appreciation of people and their development.

Better teaching is not simply the result of better technology. Rather as invitational theory points out, better teaching is a consequence of teachers who assume as a matter of course that all students are able, valued, and capable of learning important things. Such teachers maintain a people-centered orientation rather than a machine or instrumental orientation when dealing with their students, especially in technologically-mediated or virtual environments of on-line education.

Being Imaginative: What Does an Inviting Online School Environment Look Like?

A prudent approach to technology in education begins by being intentional and becoming informed. Moving forward means being inviting and integrative in our approaches to applying and using on-line technologies in our schools. But how can we move forward with technology if we cannot see where we are going or what we want to achieve? We can begin the process of moving forward by "Imagineering" our goals and dreams. Let us imagine two schools that are both inviting and prudent about their use of technology for teaching and learning.

A High Tech Elementary School

This elementary school is technologically advanced and administrators, teachers, and students are excited to be there, not because of the technology but because everything at this school contributes to an environment that invites personal and professional growth. The electronic sign at the front gate displays the school's logo with a motto that reads, "Ad Astra Per Ardua—To The Stars Through Hard Work." The sign has been designed to fit in nicely with the shrubs and student designed rock garden that surrounds it. The community support that helped pay for the sign is not forgotten, however. The sign's scrolling marquis spotlights corporate and community supporters, local events, and a variety of school activities and achievements including the arts, service to the community, academics, and sports. The school is electronically monitored but the sign indicating the monitor reads,

> Welcome visitors. For our students safety this school is video monitored. To better serve your needs, please follow the arrows to the main office. We look forward to meeting you.

The school has a student laptop program of which the principal is quite proud. The school's wireless Internet connection and classroom smart display technologies, makes it the envy of many other school jurisdictions and administrations but the principal realises that technology is only as good as the teachers and programs that support it. The principal is, therefore, a tireless advocate for her teachers and students. The principal believes in, and promotes, programs and policies that use the school's technology to achieve educational goals in targeted curriculum areas such as reading and mathematics where technology has been shown to make a measurable difference in students' skills and academic success. At public speaking sessions she encourages continuous community involvement in the school's decision-making process for on-line education as the key to unlocking on-line success.

The information technology officer at the school is an important link in the prudent and inviting approach to technological teaching and learning. The information officer chairs a technology committee made up of parents, teachers, and students. The committee helps administer the school's laptop program and keeps parents informed about what students are learning about technology and how parents can help at home. Some parents are involved in on-line student mentoring for homework and research projects. The IT officer's primary job description is helping teachers and students work with technology in ways that have been demonstrated to improve student academic success. One of the information technology officer's suggestions has been to introduce elements of the laptop program to younger students so the transition to the laptop classes in grade five is not a shock. and a group of teachers are pilot testing a personal digital assistant (PDA) project that uses a class set of hand-held computers to introduce basic computer use to children. Other teachers have started to use the hand held devices with their classes as well to engage students in collaborative experiential learning activities beyond the classroom because of the PDA's portability and infra-red data sharing capabilities. All students at the school are able to work with computer technology if it is needed or required. The laptop classes are arranged in collaborative learning pods where students can work together flexibly and where technology is just one alternative they can choose to complete their assignments. The school cannot afford to provide students with e-mail accounts, but teachers and parents have researched and implemented a freeware electronic bulletin board system so students in the laptop classes can use the virtual space for electronic communication and information sharing. All teachers at the school use the system to individually mentor a group of students. Students can ask their mentors academic or personal questions that they might not be able to ask in class. A school-wide committee of administrators, teachers, parents, and students planned, discussed, and developed the school's policies for using the electronic bulletin board for mentoring and within school communication.

Teachers at this school also work together in on-line learning groups for professional development and curriculum writing using the network's shared virtual spaces. They can electronically distribute and share ideas and materials for use in their classes. Students still save their work-in-progress and their final reports onto computer discs or the schools shared drive but they now hand in hard copies of their work for their teachers to evaluate. Students' concerns about "Big Brother" watching have been addressed by policy guidelines that establish students' personal on-line spaces as off limits to teachers, unless there is a compelling safety or legal reason to enter them.

Student assignments are prudently geared towards technology as well. A typical assignment might be a "webquest," to search for and critique information on a specific theme or subject on the Internet. However, teachers recognize individual student differences and intentionally build more flexibility into on-line assignments to allow all students greater choice in terms of using technology to complete their work. Comparisons of electronic sources and non-electronic sources for information are frequently part of in class discussions and presentations.

Technology is an integral part of the teaching and learning environment at this elementary school, but it is just one part of the total picture. This school has chosen people over technology as a guiding principle for integrating technology into the educational environment. The school is high tech but it is also high touch in terms of integrating technology in an environment that fosters and encourages growth, creativity, and learning.

A High Tech Secondary School

Now let us imagine a secondary school that has embraced information and communication technology. The display cases in the hallway host a variety memorabilia from all of the school's activities. Photos of graduates, students, and teachers involved in the arts, community service, the military, and a variety of occupations and professions line the walls as well. The television monitors that used to sit idle because there was not a teacher to help run the media program are now showing school and community announcements created by students with the support and guidance of a group of teachers, parents, and professionals. Announcement suggestion boxes set up throughout the school enable anyone who wants to suggest a message or idea for the broadcasts to do so. Birthdays, music suggestions, and jokes that are placed in the suggestion boxes are interspersed throughout the broadcasts.

Another group of teachers and parent volunteers has worked to develop local co-op programs that focus on working with technology in the real-world applications. Every student in the school has to complete a certain number of co-op placement hours before graduation. Students in the information and communication technology program are placed in local firms working as interns and are learning first-hand what web-designers, programmers, journalists, researchers, and others who work with technology do.

The high school has two computer labs. The smaller of the two labs is a special projects lab for everyone at the school. Copies of student and teacher computer generated art adorn the walls and two small tables with chairs arranged for group work or discussion are located in the center of the room. A large bookcase designed and built by the grade 12 construction class holds an assortment of how-to manuals and related books and magazines. There is no phone in the lab but there is a flat-bed scanner, laser printer, and a plotter to suit the multi-media production nature of the lab. Everyone is entitled to use the printer, plotter, and scanner when working in the lab. The atmosphere is comfortable and relaxed, an inviting workspace for small groups of students and teachers to plan, experiment with, and evaluate the uses of multimedia and internet technologies in the classroom and society.

The school's large computer lab is situated in the remains of the school's machine shop but students and teachers have taken time and effort to make the lab a more comfortable space. Students have painted a mural on the back wall depicting the history of computers. Large decorated rugs made by students in a weaving class hang on two other walls softening the cavernous echo that once dominated the room. The 50 computer workstations have been arranged in small circular pods throughout the large room. There is no dedicated "instructor's workstation" forcing teachers to remain at one specific area of the lab.

Long tables are arranged in various parts of the lab as quite work or discussion areas. In these areas students are allowed to play music quietly in the background as they work or talk. The lab has become a common work area for many students, even if they do not need to use the computers.

The signs in the lab reflect an inviting approach to teaching and learning. A large poster above the laser and dot-matrix printers reads, "Pre-paid Printing Accounts Available in various Amounts at the Library or Student Council. Printer Account funds go directly to the upkeep of this lab as a student resource." The computer lab "rules" represent a statement of principle that introduces a set of guidelines for working in the lab. The statement reads, "We believe that the technology in this lab is an educational tool for all of us to use. With that in mind please observe the following guidelines,"

◆ This is our lab. Lets keep it clean and orderly for all of us to use.

◆ Surf the web but please be careful, it can be hazardous out there.

◆ When a class is in progress, please use the auxiliary work areas quietly.

◆ Liquids can damage these computers, so please keep drinks on the worktables.

◆ Downloads use up space and time, so please use your disks and your time.

◆ Quiet music should not disturb anyone working in the lab.

◆ Please let the lab student supervisor know whenever problems begin to show.

The school's technology officer is a teacher who knows a lot about technology. The technology officer's job is to help teachers learn to work with technology in their subject areas. She knows that teaching about technology is not the same as teaching with technology and she strives to help teachers by making suggestions and offering support. She is a technophile who believes that technology may improve education for some, but only if teachers have the time and support needed to develop pedagogically appropriate practices and curriculum. The technology officer tries to lead by example in terms of technology so she demonstrates lessons, program ideas, and research where technology has made a difference in student learning. She likes to work one-on-one with teachers to develop individual action research plans for using technology to help students achieve measurable and sustainable academic improvement and success. Knowing that the technology officer is available and having empirical data on the beneficial results of working with technology in specific subject areas has encouraged many teachers to become better informed about teaching with technology. Some have enrolled in courses at the local university while others have become more involved in school-based groups and activities such as the media and communications club and the school's website committee.

The school's website is not solely the technology officer's responsibility. A committee of parents, teachers, and students is involved in the design, maintenance, and management of the school's website. The site promotes parent and community involvement in the life of the school and enables many parent's who could not otherwise be involved in school policy discussions to have a say about what is happening at the school. The site is highly popular with parents, teachers, and students. Like everything else at the school, involvement and communication by the entire school community has been the key to developing an inviting on-line education environment.

A Guide for Reflection and Planning
for Inviting Online Education

In invitational education, everybody and everything adds to, or subtracts from, connecting with students in meaningful ways. Ideally therefore, in on-line education the factors of people, places, policies, programs, and processes should be so intentionally inviting as to create an environment where each individual is cordially summoned to develop the full range of his or her intellectual, technical, expressive, and social abilities. Being educationally prudent about technology therefore, requires that we begin the process of integrating people and technology by looking at the current realities within a school environment. The checklist below provides an assessment guide for reflection and discussion of how a school can prudently integrate on-line technology in terms of the people, places, policies, programs, and processes that form the essential components of invitational education.

Using the Guide

This following checklist is part of a heuristic process that members of a school community, teachers, administrators, staff, students, and parents can use to intentionally integrate people and technology in an environment that informs people of their positive worth, ability, and self-directing power. Completing the checklist provides a guide for initial reflection and discussion of the kinds of imaginative acts of hope that are necessary to create and sustain on-line educational environments that invite human potential and growth within a school community.

Please mark your response to each of the statements by circling the appropriate number on the Likert scale placed beside the statement. The circled number indicates your level of agreement or disagreement with the description of the environmental situation at your school. Please keep in mind that these ratings are meant to be viewed as a starting point for discussion and not a value judgement about a particular school. Use this checklist to celebrate achievements, and to guide your reflections on new possibilities for integrating technology into inviting school environments.

Inviting On-line Schools Survey; v.1.0:

Likert Scale Rating: Strongly disagree - 1; Disagree - 2; Neither agree nor disagree - 3; Agree - 4; Strongly agree - 5.

People	1	2	3	4	5
Teachers, administrators, parents, students, and staff are informed about and involved in discussions on how Information and Communication Technology (ICT) is used at this school.					
Administrators encourage and facilitate faculty and staff professional development in working with ICT.					
Teachers express support and encouragement for all students in using ICT.					

	1	2	3	4	5
Teachers provide all students with opportunities to work with ICT and alternative methods for pursuing their academic and personal interests.					
Parents feel their ICT opinions and concerns are considered and dealt with fairly by teachers and administrators.					
Places					
Technology adds to and fits in well with the clean, well-maintained, and attractive appearance of the school.					
Networked computers are available in labs, the library, classrooms, and student work areas.					
Virtual work and communication spaces on school-based conferencing systems or bulletin boards are kept updated and provide relevant information for teachers, students, and parents.					
Work areas are well-lit, uncluttered, accesible to all, and conveniently located.					
The school's webpages present ICT policies and information in clear, accurate, and jargon-free language for all to see.					
Policies					
Teachers, students, parents, and administrators are involved in the policy development process for ICT.					
Accceptable use policies (AUPs) and general rules for ICT are clear, well-posted, and fairly administered.					
It is a school/board policy that teachers are updated, supported, and recognized for working with technology in their classes.					
School policy encourages teachers and non-teaching staff to use technology for professional development and growth.					

	1	2	3	4	5
Policy links ICT with the attainment of specific and explicit academic goals e.g. improving reading skills in grade five.					
Programs					
Technology programs at this school involve out of school experiences that link to the community and the world.					
Programs at this school encourage teachers and students to explore technology, its uses and meaning for society, from a variery of perspectives.					
Programs allow students fair and reasonable say in determining their technology choices and activities.					
Programs are planned with student interests, life and career goals, and technology skills training in mind.					
Programs are flexible and support student access to learning through a variety of ways including, but not limited to, on-line education.					
Processes					
Parents can expect a response to an e-mail or phone request within a reasonable length of time.					
Administrators and teachers routinely use ICT to communicare with parents, students, and the community.					
Teachers maintain clear and reasonable technology goals and assignments, keeping in mind student learning styles and interests.					
Teachers are available for students on-line but also before and after school in person.					
All students have the right and feel welcome to use labs and equipment when they need to.					

Inviting on-Line Schools, PDK Fastback, version 1.0, Dipetta, Novak, and Marini (2002).

Summary

Imagining an inviting on-line environment for teaching and learning is a powerful step towards making such an inviting environment a reality. Re-imagining an unintentional school environment for on-line education into an intentionally inviting environment is an imaginative act of hope. Using the checklist provided as a guide for discussion and reflection about a school's potential for inviting technology we begin to move from imaginative acts of hope to concrete steps towards achieving our educational goals. Inviting on-line education depends above all on how much commitment, and thought, people place on the democratic and democratizing possibilities that information and communication technology may make possible in teaching and learning. It is surely prudent for technophobes and technophiles living in this well-wired world to carefully examine and consider the messages that are sent and received through our ever-expanding array of information and communication technology. The inviting approach is intended to provide a prudent guide for moving from frenzy to educational fulfilment in our well-messaged world.

References

CyberAtlas. (2002). Available online at: www.clickz.com/stats, February 19.

Di Petta, T., Novak, J.M. & Marini, Z. (2001). Two dazed by IT: Gadgets, glitches and growth. *Society for Teaching and Learning in Higher Education Newsletter*, 32. September.

Di Petta, T., Novak, J.M. & Marini, Z. (2002). Inviting online education. *Phi Delta Kappa Fastback #498.* Bloomington, IN: Phi Delta Kappa Educational Foundation.

Ehrmann, S. C. (1998). Asking the right question: What does research tell us about technology and higher learning?" *Change Magazine*, March-April.

Lyman, P. & Varia, H.R. (2000). How much information? *Journal of Electronic Publishing*. University of Michigan Press. 6(2), December..

Novak, J.M. (2002). *Inviting educational leadership: Fulfilling potential* and applying an Eethical perspective to the educational process. London, UK: Pearson Education.

Novak, J.M., & Purkey, W.W. (2001). *Invitational education*. Fastback 488. Bloomington, IN: Phi Delta Kappa Educational Foundation.

Purkey, W.W., & Novak, J.M. (1996). *Inviting school success: A self-concept approach to teaching, learning, and democratic practice.* 3rd Ed. Belmont, CA: Wadsworth.

Schacter, J. & Fagnano, C. (1999). Does computer technology improve student learning and achievement? How, when, and under what conditions? *Journal of Educational Computing Research, 20*(4), 329-43.

Smerdon, B.& Cronen, S. (2000). Teachers' tools for the 21st Century: A report on teachers use of technology." Washington, DC: U.S. Department of Education; National Center for Education Statistics, September.

Wolfe, C. R., (Ed.). (2000). *Learning and teaching on the World Wide Web*. San Diego, CA: Academic Press.

Toronto Star. (2000). More Useless Information. Toronto Star Publishing, July 20.

Internet Resources for Children. (2002). ERIC Clearinghouse on Information & Technology (ERIC/IT), http://www.ericit.org/weblinks/weblinks.shtml, January.

Chapter 9

Inviting Authentic Parent Participation on School Councils

Alice Schutz, Mary-Louise Vanderlee, and Rahul Kumar

"I can't believe the way they treated me!"

This statement can be either good news or bad news. It is good news if parents are impressed by what was happening in the school and by how they were treated. It is bad news if parents were insulted by school personnel and do not desire to ever step through the school doors again. Our effort in this chapter is to identify practices that can intentionally and unintentionally invite or disinvite parent participation in schooling of their children.

Kumar, Schutz, and Vanderlee (2002) have found that the stories of parents' experiences as participants on school councils, provides a rich source of data that permits a discussion of invitational practices. We want school councils to be about good news but we also need to understand the nature of the bad news.

According to Parker and Leithwood (2000), "the complete set of organizational and social contextual variables influencing the work of school councils must be unpacked" (p. 61). This will help to identify the elements that inhibit or enhance the authentic and effective participation of parents on school councils.

Our research about school councils unpacks parental participation in terms of the basic concepts of invitational education. Our research involved the interviewing of long-term parent participants on school councils. The interviews focused on aspects related to what promoted or hindered their continued participation. The analysis of the interviews suggests that the process of participating in school councils can be viewed in terms of challenging, effective and recommended practices.

Challenging Practices

Consistent with the other findings (Parker & Leithwood, 2000) we found there are challenges that parents face when participating on school councils. Issues of power, fear, miscommunication, misunderstandings, group dynamics and commitment need to be dealt with in their various forms in order for school councils to be effective and productive.

Issues of Power

Power can be defined as the capacity to exercise control and authority. Indeed, the council is composed of members who hold and wield unequal amounts of power. Principals, for example, are ultimately responsible and accountable for proceedings of the school and they can demand and command corresponding power to bring about effective practices. If principals do not respect the members of the council by bringing only mundane issues to the agenda, or imposing their will without consultation a power imbalance occurs. Similarly, if parents come to the council with personal agendas or preconceived notions, the council body becomes impoverished in its capacity to effect change and wilts away into a superficial existence. Such imbalance in the distribution of power can foster a disinviting atmosphere or context for council members' interaction.

Power struggles can also exist between the members representing the various constituents that make up the council, for example teachers, staff, and parents. Parents for instance, have been known to withdraw from the council and its related activities when they discover they have no power to fire teachers or to further their own personal agendas. Teachers have also been heard to comment that they do not have sufficient power in either their schools or on the school councils. This could be reflective of the numbers of constituents that typically make up a school council.

Self-oriented struggles for power can separate the stakeholders (parents, teachers, administrators, support staff and students, and community stakeholder) from each other and hamper the effectiveness of the school council. Vested interests in the outcomes of any deliberations must be acknowledged from the onset so issues of power can be openly addressed. The difficulty lies in recognizing and admitting vested interest. Power struggles over vested interest can be unintentional and reflective of anxiety and fear of losing what individuals feel is important.

Fear

Fear among school council members occurs with anticipated loss of outcomes deemed to be important to the individual. Anticipated losses can be grouped under the three major stakeholders of the council; principal, teachers, and parents.

Principals are concerned with the following:

◆ Loss of face

◆ Loss of control with regard to curriculum, teacher development, administrative practices, parent participation, financial accumulation and distribution from fundraising events

◆ Loss of accountability

Teachers are concerned with the following:

◆ Lack of voices

◆ Censure

◆ Representation of fellow teachers when conflict is evident among the teachers

◆ Expertise in areas of curriculum programming

◆ Needs of all children not being met

Parents are concerned with the following:

◆ Lack of skills

◆ Lack of understanding or policy and procedures resulting from cultural differences and past experiences with
different levels of education

◆ Fear of the no win situation—being perceived as intrusive
when involved and not caring when not involved

Concerns of loss of power and fear are inextricably intertwined
with issues of miscommunication and dynamics.

Mis-communication and Mis-understanding

A considerable portion of what the school councils do is based
on effective communication. Some of the parents we spoke to said
that information distributed by the school council has failed to reach
them. This lack of communication and the process of distribution
of information from school councils by the school often results in
miscommunication which leads to strained relations and uninformed
participation of the general parent population. This results in parents
being misinformed or uninformed about issues to be discussed at the
council level and it hinders authentic and effective collaboration at the
council level. This may result in issues of fear mentioned earlier.

Along with miscommunication come struggles with jurisdiction. The perceived or actual roles that council members play
determine the dynamics of the whole group. For example teachers, who are experts on issues of curriculum, can be challenged
by parents. This becomes part of the power struggle and alters the
relationships between council members. In attempts to alleviate the
core problem of miscommunication and misunderstanding, school
council members need to be clearly informed of their obligations
and jurisdiction in a language that is transparent. In most cases
school councils are, in fact, advisory bodies, so posing situations

in which membership thinks it has a stronger role than advising will prove to be problematic and contribute to principals "losing face". This emphasizes the importance of the leadership role of the principal. Both tradition and mandate give the principal the final authority. Mandates for school councils are typically formulated to encourage a collaborative approach to produce the optimal educational experience for students. At the same time, however, the rest of the council members expect explanations when their advice does not direct the outcome of the decision. So issues of accountability arise. Moreover, the council members need more than spurious reasons for actions taken that are not consistent with the advice once an issue has been brought to the council. The ultimate accountability rests on the shoulders of the principal. So while the intention of the mandate to establish school councils provides the theoretical and compositional recommendations, practice confounds the process and often produces its own constraints often resulting in aspects of fear.

Dynamics

Dynamics are the forces that underlie the relationships between the participants on the council. Dysfunctional group dynamics can lead to the erosion of trust, care and optimism. Private agendas can steer a meeting into trivial issues that disenfranchise the members, resulting in an emerging gap between the factions of the school council members. For example, when grievances pertaining to the children of council members are brought to the table, and the role of the school council is reduced to that of a grievance body, all other valid issues are pushed to the side, parents are forced to choose sides, staff and principals become defensive, student confidentiality is compromised, and council effectiveness diminished. When this occurs, the enriching principles of trust, care and respect promoted by invitational theory (Novak, 2001) are disrupted. Personality and interaction style of the various members of the council affect the dynamics of the process. Issues such as the leadership style of principals and chairs can either ignite or disarm problems. For example, a chair of council who is too autocratic may silence and marginalize weaker, less confident members and the direction they might propose.

The agenda and the time and place for meetings also might challenge group dynamics. For example, if the agenda is set either by chairs or the principal without the contributions of other members and is distributed at the meeting, there are no opportunities for members to prepare thoughtful or considered reactions to those agenda items. The parents feel unprepared and isolated and often disengage from conversation and withdraw from active participation. These behaviors may then give rise to perceptions of fear, lack of skills, and lack of understanding of policy and procedures which may then perpetuate disengagement and withdrawal from active participation. When this occurs, a small committed group may take over the affairs of the council and then leads to elitism and eventual burnout.

Commitment

When the council acts as an elitist or exclusive group it can become quite powerful and dictate the directions of the school. This is problematic because parent participation becomes limited and narrows the focus and the continuity of the council. This further perpetuates feelings of inadequacy in other potential council members. Even when the council members are collegial and united in their goals, they can suffer from burnout due to the dedication and energy required to fulfill the expectations of the school community. Many of our parents spoke about the tremendous effort required to work on council and the personal sacrifices they made to do so.
In all cases where these dynamics are present, the council becomes an insignificant part of the school culture. Hence, the challenging practices that need to be considered are as follows:

◆ Power Struggles

◆ Fear associated with each of the roles of council constituents

◆ Miscommunication between and among members

◆ Dynamics—relationships and tasks among members

◆ Commitment

Participants repeatedly stated that the above concerns proved to be the major challenges associated with effective council practice.

Effective Practices

We were encouraged when our participants reported that they had been invited to participate on the council and that they consider the personal invitation as the most effective means of involving other parents in the work of the council. They insist that the council must be inclusive, democratic, accountable, and visible. They believe that some of the best ways in which this could be accomplished is through leadership training, establishing transparent processes, promotion, and inclusive and culturally sensitive communication.

Leadership Training

Many parents found the process of serving on the council quite daunting and intimidating at first. The context was new, expectations were unclear, the process was unfolding, and often members had little experience with a participatory role in the school environment.

In order to enable authentic parent involvement, a few members of the council became involved in creating and disseminating procedures and handbooks to their own and other councils in their districts. Some parents did an excellent job of documenting the process and providing the foundations for these shared documents. The documents themselves were intentionally developed to be flexible in nature so that any process identified could be modified to fit the particular situation of the various councils. The boards of education also recognized the importance of leadership training and hosted special leadership training sessions for school council members. Unfortunately, due to limited space, only one or two members of each council were invited to attend. It was up to those who did attend to disseminate the information. The leadership training sessions at the board level, while not broad, actually enhanced the roles of the attending participants to develop more inclusive training practices. Specifically it empowered those particular council members to become leaders and take on the role of council chair. Leadership training participants were then encouraged to inform other parent members of the expectations to prepare them for the role. This encouraged mentoring and validated their role contributing to personal growth. These initiatives subsequently helped them to overcome the fears associated with initial concerns of parents involving their lack of skills and their lack of understanding of policies and procedures. In addition, the preparation and subsequent confidence of the trained council members contributed to recognition from other constituents of the council including teachers and principals. This promoted a more equitable role for parents on the council and diminished some of the challenges associated with imbalance of power, vested interests, and miscommunication.

Establishing Transparent Processes

One of the items to be addressed to ensure effective transparent processes is agenda setting. Several parents explained that the process of agenda setting is crucial to the democratic and inviting nature of the council. Many stressed that such issues as who sets the agenda, how it is set, and how it is followed, dictates the effect of the council. Parents recommend that council members have the opportunity to contribute agenda items and that the final agenda be set by the chair of the council and the principal. This ensures that parents do not transcend jurisdictional boundaries by including issues that breach confidentiality, promote personal agendas, or exceed curricular mandates.

They recommended the agenda be distributed at least a week prior to the meeting so that all council members are aware and prepared for discussion at council. They stressed that when contentious issues arise, the procedures and policies set out in the handbook be used as a reference. This will prevent vested agendas from subverting the work of the council. Parents found it imperative that minutes of each meeting be made available to the school community for review so that all members of the school community could be informed and ready to participate in future meetings by being aware of the historical and precedent actions of the council.

Promotion

One of the major challenges for the council is the small number of participants willing to take on positions at the council level. One result of this situation is the burnout that is felt by those who did take part. In order to alleviate this problem, parents recommend attending all school functions to recognize and promote council membership and active participation. They stress that the personal approach, such as speaking to individual parents and identifying ways in which they could specifically contribute, is most effective. No matter how small or insignificant a contribution may seem to some—it can open the doors to greater participation, a sense of community and a bond of connection. Invitations should be addressed to both parents. Because female participation in the school has been dominant, fathers may need greater attention. Also, all new parents to a school should be contacted by phone or in person to welcome them to the school and the council members could actually provide the tour and speak about the various opportunities for involvement. Even if they cannot participate on the council itself, participation can be expanded to committees to be more inclusive. Many parents stress that one of the most effective involvement strategies emerged when they included representation from school committees such as classroom volunteers, fundraising committees, and special function organizers. Promotion of involvement also includes flyers, newsletters, and brief announcements at special events. Ensuring all parents are aware of the types of involvement is half the battle of soliciting future involvement.

Communication

As the aim of councils is to reflect the composition of the school community, and the school reflects the composition of the community in which the school is situated, methods of communication must be considerate of this composition (i.e., communication must address the languages, the level of understanding, and the perception of the invitation to participate). Councils need to know their audience and respond accordingly. In addition, they need to host their meetings in a space that reflects the invitation extended. If indeed all parents are consistently invited to attend council meetings, the space must be large enough to accommodate all those expected and invited. Therefore, our participants suggest the library, and even the cafeteria, as suitable meeting spaces. Meeting in classrooms with miniature furniture is not appropriate or appreciated, nor does it encourage future attendance.

Personal communication carries more weight than all other forms of communication combined. This is a notion that has been raised repeatedly by the parents we spoke with. It is essential to consider communication on three levels: parents at large, school community, and council. Many of the communication strategies were already discussed above but in addition such things as monitoring to make sure that communication is actually sent out by the school and received by the parents is worth mentioning. It was one of the biggest hindrances to effective practice. This means that the council must establish good communication and rapport between all members of the school community, from the secretary to the janitor. Visibility on the school premises is essential. The council members who are active and participating in the school will be taken seriously and their communication output will be given proper attention. If communication between parents and the council is to occur, such things as announcements, flyers, and space in school publication needs to be established and sanctioned by the school.

Communication also involves sensitivity to culture and language. Consideration must be placed on the way in which invitations, communications, or publications are presented in order that they do not exclude any family. In some cases this may necessitate translations. For example, in one school the newsletter was kept very factual, direct, and brief and was translated into 22 languages. Furthermore, special invitations were extended to parents who could translate to attend the meetings. This sensitivity includes the communication between members of the council as well. People will only return if they feel genuinely included and heard which means they have to have an opportunity to actively participate and share their opinions.

Effective but Non-Inviting Practices

Some of the successful practices described by the participants of the school councils appeared to fall outside the beliefs of the invitational lens and raised questions in our minds as to the influences of such practices on the ethical and democratic process.

Some very effective school council leaders believed that councils should be run like a corporation with parents being the major stakeholders in the school. Then they would have a lot more power and be effective at providing the kinds of changes which they felt to be most desirable. It made us question whether parents should move from the position of partnership to a position of power. We saw this as not being in the best interest of children, as it is a prelude to power struggles among those with the mandated power and those with acclaimed power. As well, we felt it to be an issue of equity, as those with expertise have their voices heard and those whose talents were not as well developed would surely be marginalized. We viewed this emphasis as taking away from the expertise which teachers and administrators have by virtue of their professional training being subverted by possible parental interest groups. The practice of running the school using a business model proved very effective for some councils, however for us, there are three areas of concern; power, jurisdiction and finance.

Power

Though councils were to be elected, the often low turnout led to acclaimed positions for those who show up. This process, given the business model, naturally put undue power into the hands of a minority who could impose its aims not only on other parents but on the jurisdiction of teachers and administrators. Although this doesn't happen frequently, parents can be very proud of the changes they bring about and may allow the council to run smoothly. When those chairing the council highlight issues they deem to be important, this has ramifications for future practice. For example, what if the chair is not as careful about what is highlighted, what if interpretation reflects personal agendas, what if other parents are not able to notice this? This is where we question the democracy and invitational aspect of this practice.

Jurisdiction

This became an interesting issue particularly since the governmental guidelines for councils are vague on this point. Many of the participants desired a clearer statement of jurisdiction. Parents looked to the principal to articulate this. Issues of jurisdiction that deviated from advising to that of decision-making began to appear non-inviting. Many parents wanted as one of their aims to "fire teachers." This desire to control the hiring and firing process meant that there was infringement on board and principal rights. Another contentious issue was curriculum reform. Parents may or may not know what is good for their own child, we are certain that they do not always know what is good for all children of the school. That is the domain of the teacher and principal who will view the education of all children as their main aim. This balance is in danger of being disrupted if council members are permitted an extension of their jurisdiction from advising to decision making. We question how a select group of parents can be permitted to speak for all those involved. Even elections do not address such an issue since those running may already be pre-selected in terms of ability, aim or political acumen.

Finance

A further successful, but for us non-inviting, issue centered on the issue of fundraising. This practice has long been a part of the parental contribution pattern of the school and initially was not one of the council jurisdictions. It caused some concerns, since the members who were involved in raising funds, hot dog and pizza sales, also became the members of the council. This presented some conflict of interest. However, when the councils' aims were extended to fundraising, this conflict disappeared. In most situations fundraising became a natural and accepted contribution of the council to the school. It appeared to be an area in which no resentment existed between teachers, administrators, and council members and is a very successful practice in most schools. However, fundraising can become problematic when the council's ability to generate funds results in the amassing of finances that amount to those greater than the school budget. Those who generate these finances expect to make decisions with regard to the disbursement of those funds. This interferes with the jurisdiction of the principal and raises questions such as, how does the principal maintain his role when a group was so obviously in control of the finance? What obligations would such funds demand of the teachers, principal, and board? How fair is this to other less fortunate schools? We see this as effective in terms of the goal of fundraising but non-inviting in practice as it extends the power and jurisdictional boundaries.

Recommended Practice

In summary the recommendations that reflect the invitational intentions of school councils are the following:

Equality

◆ Include and invite every parent to contribute at whatever level they can to the work of the school.

◆ Act as a bridge between the school, parents and community.

◆ Use democratic procedures and principles to ensure that the process is accountable and effective.

◆ Vary the participation process as much as possible and

continue to examine ways which make such participation equitable, representative, and encouraging.

Transparency

◆ Make the process transparent by including communication between all partners and ensuring that no rights or roles are violated.

◆ Be open to different styles of delivery, value and listen to all.

◆ Set agenda cooperatively, with enough time to respond to issues in reflective considered ways.

◆ Run meetings in such a way that the chair enacts established procedures not personal agendas.

◆ Communicate clearly, frequently, and to all, all problems, decisions, and accomplishments of the council.

Ethical Aims

◆ Value parents, teachers, principals and all other people of the school as contributors to the education of the children.

◆ Prioritize goals and initiative which respond to the needs of all involved in education.

◆ Acknowledge that volunteering is a valuable resource for the individual, the school, and the community.

◆ Stress that the council is valuable and vital as a contributing part of the education system.

◆ Examine all practices for their ethical values and discard those that are not defensible or inviting.

Training

◆ Stress that value comes through the training, mentoring, and mediating of those that know to those that are to carry on the work.

◆ Foster leadership by being knowledgeable, accessible, and encouraging to other potential candidates for council positions.

◆ Take school council initiatives and move them up to regional and national levels to promote and communicate practices that work.

Conclusion

Enlarging membership was one of the most proactive initiatives that councils could promote because it ensured the democratic and invitational nature of the school and also provided for future continuation of the council.

Given the above, council members require training in order to enable parents to get the leadership skills necessary to run the meetings and to be confident enough to understand and share their workable practices with other council members. Such things as being present and available to parents at school functions, providing handouts advertising the council in a personal approachable manner, following up with telephone conversations, and invitations and being sensitive to interest, skill, and schedules of parents all contributed to making parents feel included and valued. Others parents developed procedure manuals that made the process of conducting meetings more transparent, less daunting and more equitable. Providing a well established process also prevented council members from using personal agendas or power or from being attacked by those whose wishes were not met. The procedure became the focus not the personality.

References

Novak, J.M., & Purkey, W.W. (2001). *Invitational education*. Bloomington, IN: Phi.Delta Kappa.

Parker, K. & Leithwood, K. (2000). School councils' influence on school and classroom practice. *Peabody Journal of Education, 75*(4), 37-65.

Kumar, R., Schutz, A. & Vanderlee, M. L. (2002). Parent participation in schools and principles of invitational education. Paper presented at the American Educational Research Council, April 1-5, New Orleans, LA.

Chapter 10

Creative Primary School:
From Passion to Action

Clio Chan

Human potential, though not always apparent, is there waiting to be discovered and invited forth.

—William Purkey,
International Alliance for Invitational Education

Part 1:
The Background

Creative Primary School was founded in 1985, with a vision to create and offer the choice of an all-rounded quality education service for young students in Hong Kong.

Integrating the best of both western and Chinese educational ideas and ideals, the school strives to develop its own uniquely effective child-centered curriculum. The school aims to lay a firm foundation on which a child's future success is built during the most crucial stage of his/her development.

Creative Primary School:
Vision, Beliefs and Goals

Our *vision...*

We see ourselves as a high quality, forward thinking and inspirational learning organization—students, teachers and parents share in the joy and fulfillment of learning and achieving excellence together. With emphasis being placed on the 'education of the whole person,' we provide an ideal and happy learning environment that best promotes academic achievement fosters high values and where all students are encouraged to reach their full potential.

It is our profound *belief...*

◆ that every **child** is unique and special in his/her own way.

◆ that a child brought up in a compassionate environment learns to deal with the world positively with an optimistic attitude.

◆ that trust, encouragement and support is the foundation for building up a child's self-respect, self-worthiness and self-confidence, this in turn are the very basis for all effective learning.

◆ that **a child's development** is a summative series of breakthroughs in his/her learning process.

◆ that a child's successful and happy development is based upon his/her confidence in facing challenges, ability and persistence in problem solving, courage in accepting failure, and an accumulation of successful experiences in achievements.

◆ that during a child's primary phase of education and development is of critical importance. Individual abilities and specific needs should be properly recognized, and the most suitable level of guidance and support should be given.

Opportunities should also be constantly created for the child to experience achievements and successes.

Therefore, we *strive to* provide our students with...

◆ **a compassionate school environment**—and through a culture of care, trust, encouragement and understanding, our students learn the ways to appreciate and to gratify. With self-respect and self-worthiness, they themselves become compassionate and learn to aspire to their own ideals.

◆ **the highest standards of well-rounded care throughout the school**—and ensuring that our student's physical, cognitive, emotional and social developments are attentively looked after. Healthy, energetic, optimistic and confident, our students are professionally guided to reach their full potentials.

◆ **a stimulating learning culture**—with a uniquely developed quality curriculum reinforced by a happy and fulfilling learning environment. Assisted by a comprehensive range of information technology facilities, our students' perpetual learning habits, global out-looks, intellectual capacity, and cultural aspirations are shaped and enhanced at an early stage of their development.

◆ **an effective multi-faceted teaching approach**—which is constantly brought in line by the latest teaching theories and research. Students are inspired to develop keen interest in learning and to be proactive in the exploration of new knowledge and experience. Open-minded and far-sighted, they are encouraged to think creatively and critically at a young age.

◆ **maximum opportunities to realize own abilities and interests**—with an aim to unlock and expand all aspects of innate potentials of our students. Through both academic and extra-curricular activities, students are constantly given chances to discover their special interests and individual abilities, to challenge themselves in pursuit of excellence, and to experience the satisfaction of realizing their own aspirations and ambitions.

As a pioneer in providing quality child-centred education in Hong Kong, Creative Primary School ("CPS") has a tradition of viewing students as the most important stakeholder in making school policies, designing curriculum and implementing programs in the school. Students' best interests have always been the top priority of the school.

The ideals of the school (rather unique in the cultural setting in Hong Kong, especially during the inception of the school in the early 1980s) attracted not only parents and students, but also teachers and staff who share the same philosophy. As a result, school directors, administrators, teachers and menial staff all shares the school's mission and thus work together towards the common goals of the school. This has enabled the school to enjoy high reputation for its happy, caring and proactive approach to education since its establishment in 1985.

Students of CPS enjoy their school lives very much and have a strong sense of belonging. Moreover, its graduates are known for all-roundedness in their achievements as well as their cheerful and self-confident characteristics.

The school is blessed with a team of passionate professionals who are not only loving and hardworking, but are also very keen to learn and to innovate to improve the way students are to be educated. In fact, in the 20 years of its history, CPS has never stood still in it continuous enhancement of its approaches and methodology.

The Inception of Invitational Education

An important spark for a new level of development came in 1999 with a talk by Professor William Purkey and Professor John Novak who came to Hong Kong for an invitational education training program. We attended the talk and were extremely excited to realize that ideals of the school could be further realized through invitational education. What impressed us were not only the concept of invitational education (which is a perfect fit with the founding philosophy of the school), but also the strategies (5Ps), which can turn passions and ideals in education into actions and enable the school to develop and achieve the set of aims of the school even more effectively.

Learning More about IE

Since then, effort has been made to learn more about invitational education. Principal and teachers tried to attend every seminar and workshop on invitational education, and exhausted different means, such books and the World Wide Web to learn more about it. Besides that, the school invited an officer of the then Education Department ("ED") Mr Peter Wong who was sent to follow Professor Purkey for attachment to conduct a school director-administrator-teacher-staff training workshop on invitational education. Touched by the potential positive effects of IE on students, we became serious about putting theories of IE into practice. The more we learnt about IE, the more determined we were to become a truly inviting school. We then began to infuse the ideas of IE into the daily life in the school through the 5 Ps: People, Places, Policies, Programs and Processes.

Support

Full support not only came from teachers and staff, parents and students were also very happy to see the measures we took in terms of the 5Ps to make the school an even better place to study in. The School Board was very supportive. They decided to include invitational education as one of the main themes for school development. They also approved of releasing my immediate duties (I was the vice principal of the school at that time) and sponsored me to attend the IAIE World Conference in 2000 in Lexington, Kentucky and to visit about twenty inviting schools in the US.

The 2000 IAIE Conference and After

The conference and the school visits all proved to be very inspiring and rewarding. During the 17-day study trip I experienced a lot of care and support from educators around the world who shared the same ideals, learned a lot more about IE and witnessed how the plans and theories of IE had been put into action.

After I returned to Hong Kong, a sharing session about the study trip was organized in the school. A presentation with more than two hundred slides and video clips were shown. At the same time, a report with a list of recommendations based on the collective ideas of colleagues under the 5Ps on developing IE in school were drawn up. The report was sent to the School Board and it was endorsed unanimously.

In order to encourage participation in creating an even more inviting school, we tried to involve everyone in the staff in brainstorming on things we can do in different aspects to bring about an inviting school. Blessed with the unique school culture at CPS, teachers and staff are particularly devoted and keen to learn. Each functional group[1] soon reached consensus on how to proactively integrate the recommendations into their yearly plans.

Again, thanks to the enthusiasm and hard work of all staff in planning and monitoring the implementation of IE through the 5Ps, we have received very positive feedback from students and parents on what we have done. The results of the Inviting School Checklist also confirmed that IE really worked well in our school.

In 2002, Creative Primary School was presented the Inviting School Award by the International Alliance of Invitational Education in recognition of our effort and achievements in providing an inviting school environment for our students. This was a great encouragement to all at CPS.

Now the spirit of IE is well embedded in our school culture, system and policies. However, we dare not be complacent about this because we believe that as a learning organization, there is still a lot that we can do to further our educational ideal and empower each of our students to unlock their boundless potential.

Part 2:
Invitational Education in CPS—the 5 Ps

People

One very important aspect of IE is its highlight on **Intentionality**. It is a profound belief of IE that every member in the school is valuable, responsible and possesses boundless potentials. Everyone in the school including students, teachers, other staff, and parents, even visitors are expected to be treated with respect, trust, and care. In order to create this atmosphere, we have intentionally done a lot to make people understand that they are respected, trusted, cared for and possess boundless potentials.

Passionate Professionals

As our school is set up with an aim to provide high quality education that emphasizes care and joy in learning, it attracts dedicated teachers and other staff with the same aspirations. In order to ensure high quality of the team, we place great emphasis on the recruitment process. Great care is also put in to ensure there is a match of ideals and competence. A mentor system where new teachers are teamed up with experienced teachers is used to make certain that the new teachers adapt well to our unique school culture.

Staff development for new and existing teachers as well as other staff is a vigorous ongoing process that consists of workshops, talks by prominent educators and childhood psychologists and the regular Staff/ Curriculum Development Days. In this way, our team members not only possess the passion, but the knowledge and skills to strive for an ideal environment to enable everyone's potentials to be developed to their full.

We consider the staff of the school as the key to whether the ideals of the school can be achieved in practice. In line with the philosophy of IE, we believe that each and every staff member possesses unique potentialities waiting to be unlocked. Therefore, every effort is made to encourage teachers and other staffs to develop and challenge themselves in realizing their potentials. We take special care to make known to individual teachers and staff how we appreciate their potentials and strengths that we observed, and are always ready to encourage them to develop themselves in an area/ areas where they can become a specialist. We also provide them with opportunities and give them enough support as they work towards their goals.

The relationship among colleagues is very close. This is not just because teachers all sit in one staff room or that they prepare lessons in teams, organize activities in teams, and do projects in teams. Actually, many are attracted to the school by its unique ideal in education and are all very committed towards their profession. They work late together; face the daily challenges together; sharing tears and laughter. Respect, care, trust, and eventually mutual support among the CPS team are thus grounded on a solid foundation that is developed organically. With this atmosphere, optimism also tends to persist as colleagues are sure that they will be looked upon by colleagues positively and that their team is always behind them.

People working at CPS including school managers, principal, teachers, receptionists, clerks, and even menial staffs enjoy working here. The rate of staff turnover is very low. Very often, teachers who leave the school for studies often choose to come back to work for the school again after his/ her studies finish. Everyone sees himself/ herself as having a role in the school and feels that his/ her work is meaningful.

Each Child Is Uniquely Valuable

In the school, each student is regarded as unique, with their special talents. Teachers do not just consider themselves as experts in transmitting knowledge. They always have the child at heart and actively identify potentials of each and every child. They will then encourage them and provide opportunities for them to develop such talents and potentials to the full.

In our school, every teacher is also a counselor to the pupils. Teachers are sensitive to pupils' emotions and special needs. We have a very strong guidance team. The team not only arranges workshops for teachers to improve their knowledge on child development and counseling, but they also run personal development camps for pupils so that pupils learn to deal with difficulties and challenges positively.

It is very important to let students know that how much they are valued and loved, so that they learn to value and love themselves. Here, I think the principal has a special role to play: the principal is regarded by most children as a powerful figure in the school. Thus, I intentionally made use of this image to make maximum impact on students' self image: I make use of every opportunity to get close to my students and know each of them personally: I greet the students when they come to school, say goodbye to them when they leave school, pay special attention to their expression to see if they are happy and well. I visit my students all the time, take active part in their activities, and observe them at recess. I arrange students to chat with me in my office, take photos with together, and try to remember each student's name (although there are more than seven hundred students in the school, and I am not able to remember all the names most of the time). I always tell them my expectations on them while at the same time tell them how special they are, how much I care about them, and how happy I am to be their principal. In this way, they would appreciate that they are valued as an individual even by someone whom they regard as a VIP so that their self-image and self-confidence can be enhanced significantly.

Pupils: Making All Our Efforts Worthwhile

Under this caring environment, pupils understand that they are respected, trusted, invited and cared for. They consider the school their other home and they know they are valued as individuals. Smiling faces are everywhere. Teachers need not use their authority to "control" the students because they know how much teachers love them so they are willing to cooperate. They are not afraid of teachers. Instead, they respect and love them. They understand the high expectation placed on them by the teachers stem from teachers' concern for the students' own welfare.

Pupils of CPS are generally very well behaved. The sense of belonging is strong. They are proud of being a member of the school. Every morning, pupils and teachers gather together in the playground. When there are challenges ahead for someone in the school (e.g., when students of the highest form are going to take a very important examination soon and there is anxiety, or when someone is seriously sick) everyone in the playground will pray together. When it is announced that the school gets good achievements or prizes from outside competitions, everybody in the playground cheers. When our school team loses in a competition, everybody in the playground will express their care and support towards the team members and the teachers who are in charge of the team, and let them know the whole school is behind them.

Because the sense of belonging is strong, pupils here tend to have very good relationships with each other. We stress that students should behave well to and take care of each other like brothers and sisters. We have also intentionally create lots of opportunities for pupils to play and work together regardless of their class and forms, most pupils have lots of friends in different classes and grades. Pupils in the higher forms are considered as big brothers and sisters who would care for those in the lower forms.

Parents: Our Unfailing Supporters and Partners

Parents are our closest partners. Through talks, seminars, Parents' Day, very frequent circulars to parents and a lot of informal communications such as face-to-face chats or phone calls and many other parent-students activities, we have successfully fostered two-way communication with parents. This mutual understanding and coordination has meant that there is close collaboration between parents and the school in the education of students.

We also have a very active Teacher Parent Association. Parents and teachers often work hand in hand in organizing activities for the students, helping the individual children with difficulties and so on. Parents are very happy to contribute their expertise in assisting in school functions. Last year, we had more than one third of parents contributed as parent volunteers in various school/ PTA activities.

Like teachers, many parents who share the same education beliefs are attracted to bring their children to study in our school. This magnet effect is getting increasingly obvious. Last year, Dr. Roger Chen, an education expert in Thinking Education and Value Education working in a university in Hong Kong came to visit our school to share his expertise on this special area. We had a great time-sharing our beliefs and ways of implementation. After a few days, he called and inquired about the procedure of admission into our school because he would like his kid to receive the education we provide too. He was now one of our parents, and had worked closely with the school to develop a thinking program in the school to enhance the thinking education in our school. There are many similar incidents happening in our school, thus bringing in lots of additional resources and insights into the school.

We are very open to parents' suggestions and advice, because we consider their voice very important and relevant to the improvement of the school. We share mutual strengths and support to lead our students towards academic success and other achievements. Teacher-parent relationship is very good and trusting. Results from parents' surveys we conduct twice a year confirm that more than 90%, less than 1 % rate us dissatisfactory. We understand that it is very hard to keep all parents satisfied in every single aspect of the school, as sometimes the requests are contradictory. But we still value the voice of every parent, and try to cater for individual needs. While we stress that we welcome parents' advices, we also ask parents to give us encouragements. These encouragements are very important because they spare us from burning out and give us confidence, drive and strength we need to keep moving towards our goals and aims.

Places

Hong Kong is a very small and crowded place. Schools in general are small, compact and old. Our school premise was built in 1960 and is small in size too. We do not have a big lawn or a beautiful playground. But despite all these limitations, we have strived to make the school place pleasant and comfortable.

The building and ground of our school have always been well maintained, clean and well lit. Classrooms are decorated with different color schemes and children's work and achievements have been prominently displayed both inside and outside classrooms. It has also been well equipped with the facilities that suit modern teaching requirements. The School Board is very supportive and has put in much resource to upgrade the equipment to this end. When compared with facilities of other schools in Hong Kong, ours are already rather advanced and well kept. And before we were introduced to invitational education, we thought this was already sufficient.

After meeting Professor Purkey and Novak in 1999, we began to realize that a lot can be/ should be done in order to be an inviting school. In-house IE workshops stimulated every member of the staff to think about ways to make our school setting more inviting. As a result, lots of good suggestions were received. The trip to attend IAIE World Conference in 2000, 2002, 2004 and visits to more than twenty inviting schools in North Carolina, Kentucky, and Ohio definitely gave us a lot of inspirations as well. We learned how to use "places" to create powerful influence on and satisfaction for people.

Since then, lots of efforts were put into creating an inviting environment for a caring, warm, attractive, aesthetic and interesting school environment in which people can be inspired, motivated and feel invited.

We think to be inviting, the school must give everybody a genuine impression that the school is welcoming. The school reception area must be a warm and inviting place. One of our school managers (who is an architect himself and an advocate of invitational education himself) volunteered to redesign the setting of the office, the reception area as well as the classrooms in the school.

Attractive banners are hung up in various places in the school. Enlarged photos of our students, plaque of our school vision, trophies and awards earned by the students are all displayed in prominent places in the school. Posters with positive messages and encouragements, which motivate students, are posted throughout the premise. We tried every effort to make use of the place to remind ourselves as well as the students the value we uphold all the time.

In order to make the office even more inviting to pupils, part of the counter is lowered to allow children from the lower forms to communicate with the office. We also use living plants and soft toys to make the office cozy and refreshing. In order to create a comfortable and convenient environment for teachers, we also renovate and refurnish the staff room. We encourage teachers to decorate their own seat with a personal touch too.

Apart from that, our library is renovated so that it is more comfortable and can let more natural light in. The opening of the library is also extended to maximize its use. We also try to use banners, color flags, living plants etc. to make the school more lively and attractive. Old and worn out furniture was replaced.

In order to enhance students' love towards their classes, we asked parents, pupils and teachers to join efforts in decorating the classrooms with their own mat, cushions, festive decorations, and favorite toys to make their classroom personal and homely. We also post a happy class photo outside their classroom to remind them the classroom belongs to them.

Our experience in improving the "places" element in our school in the past few years is very encouraging. We now appreciate a lot more the importance of making the school environment inviting. Besides cleanliness and good maintenance, the school has now become even more attractive. The atmosphere is even more cheerful, welcoming, and cozy. Yet we are not going to stop here. We will continue to pool ideals both from inside and outside of school to make the school an even more inviting and happy place for everyone in the school.

Policies

In our school, pupils should be central to everything we do. Policies in the school is therefore written to make sure that people in the school understand and follow this direction. We draw up these policies not only for the present good of the students. We also try to be forward thinking so that the policies we wrote down are beneficial to students' future life.

Policies in the school are compiled and presented in the form of guidelines and manuals. These policies are prepared by the school management team, which comprises of the principal, vice principals, teachers in charge of different functional groups, as well as different subject panels in the school. The functional groups include the Curriculum Development Team, Counseling Team, Discipline Team, Extra-Curricular Activities Development Team, Team for Student Matters & Parents Liaison, IT Team, Team for General Matters and Team for Crisis Management. Every teacher in the school belongs to at least one functional group based on their interests. They are encouraged to take part in suggesting and reviewing the policies every year and in planning for the coming year. The policies are thus a product of concerted efforts of the whole staff in the school.

Some of the important policies of our school include:

1. Policies on Teaching and Learning:

◆ Our curriculum should cater for the present as well as future needs of the students. We should be active in learning about the latest developments in education, theories and researches in child psychology, brain studies, childhood development, recommendations and guidelines from the local education authority, as well as social development of Hong Kong and China. And regularly reviewed our curriculum so as to ensure that our curriculum is forward thinking and is able to meet the overall needs of our students.

◆ Our curriculum should be broad and balanced so that our students will receive a whole person education. We should make sure that our students are well looked- after intellectually, emotionally, psychologically, socially, physically and spiritually.

◆ Our curriculum should be child-centered and cater for the interests of our students. Teachers are encouraged to make use of various approach of teaching to motivate the students to learn proactively.

◆ Our curriculum should be challenging enough to encourage students stretch their ability and stimulate students' high order thinking.

◆ Our curriculum is able to develop students learning skills and habits so that students are able to apply their knowledge with skills and flexibility.

◆ Tests and examinations are not the ultimate aims of learning. We should focus on reviewing whether students have mastered key elements in the learning process and are able to apply what they have learnt. Therefore, we should engage ourselves in continuous assessment to monitor students' academic progress, and make sure that their specific performances are reported frequently to parents. That is, the report would include not just the overall grade of the assessment but also the level of competence and knowledge in specific areas of the curriculum. That way, the assessment becomes more of a tool for continuous improvement, rather than as an end in itself.

◆ The main purpose of homework is to reinforce what the pupils have learnt and also to let pupils appreciate the importance and uses of what he/ she has learnt. The homework, therefore, should be appropriate in length, interesting, meaningful and stimulating.

◆ We should respect individual differences. Special assistance should be given to pupils with special needs, especially those with learning difficulties and those with special talents and gifts. We should not label pupils according to their present performance. Therefore, we should not release pupils' overall ranking in examinations so as to avoid unhealthy competition among pupils.

2. Policies on Untapping Pupils' Potential:

◆ Every staff should be sensitive to pupils' individual interests, strengths and weaknesses, and encourage pupils to discover and further develop their talents.

◆ It is our responsibility to provide a diverse range of learning experiences by organizing various extra-curricular activities for students so that they can have opportunities to participate in a great variety of activities. These activities should be able to unlock students' potentials, to develop confidence, teamwork skills, creativity, leadership, self-discipline and initiative and to widen their horizons.

◆ We should intentionally provide opportunities for members in the school to exhibit their talents.

◆ In order to encourage pupils to work on their strengths, recognition should be given when they put in their efforts. Therefore we should be generous in giving pupils awards and certificates.

3. Policies on Child development, Discipline and Counseling:

◆ As the primary school years constitute the critical period when a child's personality, character and value systems are formed. We should therefore devote major attention and effort to ensure that our students receive the best guidance in these areas of development.

◆ Every member in the staff should be responsible for students' healthy development during different stages. In-house counseling services and referral should be provided for students with needs. Positive activities to help students cope with the challenges with regards to growing up and changes, and activities to widen students' exposure and experience in dealing with difficulties in a positive manner should be arranged.

◆ As for discipline, we should adopt a constructive and positive method. Our staff should be open-minded and trusting, helping our students to be self-motivated at all times. We should emphasize encouragement rather than reprehension and punishment, and positively guide students towards self-discipline. To understand, demonstrate, advice, encourage and support is more effective in changing pupils' behavior than to blame and scold. We should also make use of every opportunity to promote, encourage, and provide training in self-discipline, respect and concern for others, and development of desirable moral standards.

4. Policies on Professional Development of Staff:

◆ Our school should be an energetic, progressive and learning organization. We regard professional development as a continuous process that should be attended to constantly.

◆ We regard information from self-evaluation and appraisal positive means to further improve oneself in the process of professional development.

◆ We intend teachers to participate in discussions on school matters and share views on the improvement of the school.

◆ We encourage teachers to learn from each other and make learning a lifelong quest.

◆ We invite teachers to identify areas they want to become expert of and give support according.

5. Policies on School-Parent Relationship:

◆ We should work in close collaboration with parents through frequent informal communication and regularly organized functions such as seminars, Parents' Days and many other parent-students activities and share mutual strengths and support to lead our students towards academic success and other achievements.

◆ We should take parents views and opinions serious and positively.

◆ Parents are our closest partners in overall development of the school. We should create more opportunities to discuss school matters with parents, and encourage parents to participate in the teaching, learning and other school activities.

◆ The Parent-Teacher Association should be an important (though not the only) means through which we can further the collaboration and cooperation between the school and parents.

Programs

As "programs" are very effective means to realize the concept of invitational education, we have designed and implemented a large number of programs to facilitate pupils' learning and personal development, teachers' personal and professional developments as well as parents' education and involvement in the school.

The followings are examples of these programs:

1. Programs Related to Formal Curriculum

Curriculum Development Projects

Through the years, our school has the tradition to engage in curriculum development years after years and resulted in many new initiatives. Many of such efforts are unique in Hong Kong at the time of their introduction. As such initiatives have important implication to the overall educational process experienced by the children; we have a special functional group (the Curriculum Development Committee) that is responsible for reviewing the curriculum from time to time. Their role is to enhance the quality of learning and teaching to make sure that our curriculum is in line with relevant theories and research in child psychology and childhood development, the latest developments in educational theories and methods, as well as recommendations and guidelines from local education authority of Hong Kong.

Through the years, the committee has taken the lead in creating and developing a student centered Curriculum and school-based new subjects such as Computer-Assisted Learning for Chinese, English and Mathematics (introduced in 1989), Native English Speaker Teaching Program (introduced in 1993), Computer Awareness Programs at the Primary School Level (introduced in 1994) and "EQ & Thinking Course" (introduced in 1997) has been included in the formal curriculum.

Besides that the committee also incorporates new effective teaching approaches as well as strategies into the curriculum, these approaches include "Sheng Boon Approach of Education" (introduced in 2002), Thinking Education (introduced in 2003) and Brain-based Learning (introduced in 2004). In view of the increasing importance of Putonghua for communication inside China, we start to offer choices for students to learn Chinese through Putonghua or Cantonese. We also see the increasing needs of students to use English worldwide; we are going to switch the medium of instruction in certain subjects such as Bible Studies and Science to English.

In 2001, the school started a 5-year curriculum development project, inviting scholars and experts to work side-by-side with teachers. The review undertaken this time has as one of its focuses the inspiring and development of students' potentials. Results of this project not only further enhance curriculum content and teaching strategies but also equip teachers with expertise in curriculum planning and development. This in turn also significantly fosters professional growth / development of the staff.

Year-Round Programs

Every year, a theme is chosen for the school as the theme for the Year-round Program. These themes are usually chosen with reference to the current issues in Hong Kong and the changing needs of pupils in mind. For Example, in 1997-98, when Hong Kong's sovereignty was returned to China, we introduced the Year-round Program " Chinese Heart, Global Mind" in order to prepare pupils for the new identity ahead. After that, we had Year-round Programs such as "The Joy of Learning," "The loving Heart," "The Love for Life," "Welcoming the new millennium," "Team Work," "Having

Fun in Reading," "Be Proactive in Learning," and " 5E: Enjoying English, Experiencing English, Exploring in English and Excelling in English."

Creative Week Programs

Thinking power is one of the areas which teachers can work on in order to unlock students' full potential. Therefore, one study week is set aside to focus on thinking education. Teachers of the whole form will select a broad theme for students to work on. They will introduce and weave in elements of thinking education (for example, the ACCESS Thinking Strategies of Dr. Roger Cheng) in its design. During this week, students will get into groups, take the initiative to choose a topic for their project, experience different processes such as problem/ question analysis, creation of solutions/ answers, critique of solutions/ answers, explication of the problem solving/ question-answering process, sentimental reflections on problem solving/ question-answering process and synthesis of the problem solving/ question-answering process. On the final day of the week, the school will be open to parents and outsiders and the students will demonstrate or perform what they have created in this special week to visitors.

Exchange Programs

To broaden students' perspective so that they can have a global view, we have organized various exchange programs either with overseas schools or schools in Mainland China. Such programs could take various forms. Sometimes, we might send teachers and students to an overseas school and place them in the daily routine of that school. In return, teachers and students from our counterpart will be placed in our school in the same way. At other times, we may organize study tours when a group of teachers, parents and students would visit a certain locality in mainland China or overseas and visit several schools there. Seminars, sharing and performances are usually organized so that teachers, students and other members of the schools can learn more from each other.

Enrichment Programs

As every pupil is special and unique in their own ways, teachers in our school have implemented a number of programs so as to assist pupils with various needs. The followings are some of the enrichment programs in our school:

◆ We invite pupils who need special assistance in learning Chinese, English and Mathematics to join **Study Groups, Study Camps** and **Learning for Fun Programs** where teachers can do remedial in small groups and play learning games with pupils so that pupils will not lose interest in learning the subjects they find difficult.

◆ We also organize seminars and workshops for teachers and parents so that possible learning or behavioral problems can be identified and tackled in time.

◆ We invite pupils with special talents to join the **"Project A" Program** in which children of higher abilities can come together to participate in challenging activities in which they stimulate each others' intellectual abilities and talents under the facilitation of teachers.

◆ Because of the nature of the subject Mathematics, we notice that when pupils progress to P.5 and 6, there is often some who performs significantly better than required by the normal curriculum. So we have a new program named **Accelerated Mathematics Learning Groups** for such pupils with outstanding achievements in Mathematics. The responses of pupils, teachers and parents are very good.

◆ We also introduce ability group teaching in English at high forms when the range of standard in English widened.

2. Programs for Personal Development, Character Training, and Moral Education

As primary school years are the critical period when a child's personality, character and value systems are formed, we have implemented many programs to ensure our pupils' healthy development. The following are some of these programs:

◆ Award Program—to encourage and give formal recognition to pupils' good behaviors. Such awards include for example, Service Award, Merit Awards, Improvement Awards, Model Students, and Award for Excellent Conduct, Outstanding Student Awards, etc.

◆ Personal Growth Program—to offer well structured personal growth programs for each form. Theme for individual forms include:

◆ "Smooth Transition into Primary School" for Primary 1
◆ "Learning to be Self Discipline and Responsible" for Primary 2
◆ "Mastering Social Skills" for Primary 3
◆ "Embark on Creativity" for Primary 4
◆ "Enjoying Voluntary Services" for Primary 5
◆ "Leadership Training" for Primary 6

◆ Smooth Transition Program—principal invite P.1 students to visit her office and tell her how they feel about their school life; counselor and principal chat with every new student to the school to make sure they settle down well in CPS.

◆ Love from the Upper Form Program—this includes the Big Brother and big sister Program, the Caring Ambassador Program. We encourage upper form students to look after the lower form students.

◆ Challenge Camp Program—to encourage pupils to face challenges with confidence, perseverance and equip them with teamwork and problem solving skills

3. Programs to Unlock Pupils' Potentials

Each year we organize a large number of activities both in the formal and informal curriculum for students to develop their potentials. Students have lots of opportunities to participate in a large variety of such activities inside as well as parties outside the school. The following are some of these programs:

◆ Special Events in the School Calendar—each year we have Sports Day, Swimming Gala, Musical Instrument Competitions, Singing Competitions, Ball Games Competitions, Writing Competitions, Drawing Competitions, Mathematics Competitions, General Knowledge Competitions, Design Competitions, Project Competitions etc. to stimulate pupils' interests and offer opportunities for pupils to discover and recognize their own special talents. We intentionally increase the number of winners so that more pupils can have the chance to get recognitions.

◆ Talents Spotting Program—Class teachers and subject teachers will observe the students and fill in a form to report to parents on their observation regarding individual potential and talents of each child in the class.

◆ Lunch Time Talent Show—Students are intentionally invited to perform/ show their talents after their lunch. Others students will come to the Hall to be the audience and cheers for their schoolmates.

◆ School Team and Outside School Activities and Competitions—for pupils with special talents in various fields, teachers will offer special trainings to the students and encourage the students to take part in activities and competitions outside school so as to broaden their horizons. Examples of these training programs include: School Choir, School Band, School String Orchestra, School Verse Speaking Team, School Art Team, School IT Team, School Mathematics Team, School Dance Team, School Swimming Team, School Athletics Team, School Basketball Team, Volleyball Team, Mini-Tennis Team, Table-Tennis Team, Badminton Team Training etc.

◆ Friday Afternoon Programs—there are over 30 kinds of activities which pupils can choose from according to their own interests. Examples of these activities include: Bread Making, Drama, Western Cooking, Calligraphy, Ball Games, Model Making, Creative Show, Philately, Verse Speaking and Painting, etc.

◆ Multiple Intelligence Enhancement Programs—for pupils who want to further develop their interests. Examples of these activities include: Musical Instrumental Classes, Swimming, Chinese Kung Fu, Board Games, Creative Writing, Gymnastics, and English Oral Classes, etc.

◆ Community Services and "Uniformed Groups"—such as Girl Guide, Boy Scout, Environmental Ambassadors for pupils to learn about social values, team work, self-discipline and to render services to others.

◆ Student Ambassador Program—to encourage students to care for, know more about the school and represent the school to receive guests.

◆ PTA Scholarship Program—Scholarships donated by Parent-Teacher-Association to recognize students who have excellent achievement in the sports, arts or social services donates scholarship for Sports, Arts and Social Services.

◆ Creative Students On Stage Variety Show—Students would occupy centre stage and perform in grand theatre such as the City Hall in front of a large audience of over 1,000 consisting of fellow students, parents and even friends.

4. Programs of Staff Development

Staff development is considered an important means to improve the quality of education services in school. We have, thus implemented the following programs:

◆ Continuous Professional Training Program—we encourage every member of the staff to enroll in seminars and workshop offered by the Education and Manpower Bureau ("EMB") and other professional institute and bodies. A budget is set aside to sponsor teachers to pursue further professional development.

◆ In-house staff training—Each year, we have a Staff Development Day Camp (for team building and professional development), a Curriculum Development Day (for curriculum review and development in subject groups), three to four teachers' seminars and workshops (on teaching methods and techniques, e.g., Mind Mapping).

◆ Mentor Program—Experienced teachers taking care of the less experienced teachers.

◆ Sharing Program—Opportunities for teachers share knowledge, expertise with each other. Examples of such activities may include:

> ◆ A teacher who is good at IT may be invited to share his/ her strategies in using IT in teaching with other teachers.

> ◆ A subject panel may invite teachers to sit in his/ her classroom.

5. Programs for Parental Involvement and Education

Parental involvement and education is one of the main focuses of programs that our school is keen to develop in the past few years. The following are some of these programs:

◆ School-Parents Communication Program—Apart from using school handbooks (when weekly/daily notes on observations about the child's behaviour are often exchanged), school circulars, newsletter, Parent's Guide, school web to communicate with parents, parents are encouraged to communicate with the school by phone, by fax, by email or in person. We encourage parents to come to our school not only on Parents Days but also at other times. We always ask for parents' comments and suggestions through formal questionnaires and informal dialogues to improve our service.

◆ Parent-Teacher Association—The association provide the opportunities for parents and teachers to meet nearly every month to work collaboratively for the good of the pupils. The association also helped organizing joint school-parent programs and activities such as Gatherings, Outings, Overseas Study Trips, and Scholarship Program for Talented Students, etc.

◆ Parent Support Groups—Under the PTA, we have three support groups from parents to assist in curriculum development in the school, to advice on and promote pupils' healthy living style and diet, and to publish newsletter for the association.

◆ Parental Involvement Program—where parents are invited to participate the school events (such as in the Swimming Gala, Sports Day, Music Camp, Flower Charity Day, Social Services etc.) and to be involved in the school as volunteers in school activities (e.g., as photographers on Sports Days, as Reading Dad/ Mom in the Reading Award Scheme, as guest speakers in certain teaching and learning activities).

◆ Parent Education Program—Every year, we have at least two Seminars for parents from every form. Apart from that we also have workshops for parents for different classes and parents of different needs.

Processes

Processes at the school are characterized by openness, liveliness, mutual support and respect for everybody in the school. The following are some of the examples of how our processes are inviting:

◆ Morning Music—Every morning when students arrive

the school, they will be greeted by lively music broadcast in the whole school. This provides an energetic beginning to the school day. Music for concentration is also played before tests and exams to help students relax, as well as improve their performance.

◆ Respect for everyone's ideas—Ideas and opinions of students are respected, even actively sought out. For example, when the school was looking for a mascot, students were first invited to give their ideas. Their great response testifies to their trust that they opinion will be taken seriously. Everyone in the school including students, parents, teachers, principal, school directors and menial staff are invited to vote for their favorite mascot. The most popular mascot was eventually adopted.

◆ Women/ Men in Red—A way to show support to each other in the school. For example, when the English Team launched a special English Day Program, all English teachers wore red clothes. Other non-English teachers showed their support by wearing red clothes on that day as well.

◆ Sports Days for everyone—The annual Sports Day is not just an occasion for sports competitions. Actually it is a chance to have fun together for everyone including students, parents, teachers, principal and menial staff. For example, there are competitions among teams formed by parents and their kids. Also, every year, a cheering team performance is designed and staged by students, teachers and parents. The principal joined the cheering dance too.

◆ Variety of learning methods—At CPS, teachers use a great variety of methods, and provide different learning environments to stimulate students' learning. They include various activities inside the classroom, visits outside of school, special events, drama, competitions, projects, talks by outside experts, etc.

◆ Words to show one cares—Notes and memos showing mutual care is often exchanged between teachers, between teachers and students and between parents and teachers. One could find them stuck to the daily sign-in sheet, on one's desk (with some snack), among the exercise books, etc.

◆ 360 degree appraisals—The 360 degree method for performance evaluation is adopted so that superiors, peers as well as subordinates get to give suggestions and comments on how one is performing. Even the principal is opened to be appraised by the other staff.

To conclude, we are fortunate to have developed a culture that is dynamic, open, that is also trusting, caring and fun. This has ensured both efficient and effective implementation processes, which are well coordinated. The dynamic and open atmosphere ensures that problems are spotted and discussed in the open and solutions are suggested and given full considerations. The strong trust and genuine care born out of a shared philosophy, mutual understanding and most important of all, the experience of working and overcoming challenges together have ensured that discussions, debates and differing opinions can be dealt with without detrimental effects on team work and unity.

Part 3:
Unending Quest

What we have presented above is a report on the match of educational philosophies and approaches of creating primary schools and invitational education and how invitational education is implemented in our school. We are always very encouraged by the achievement of our students who show significant changes and developments after they have joined the "creating primary school family." However, despite such accomplishments, we are sure that we have many challenges to face everyday; and there are always things that we can do better; things we have not done enough. In fact, it is this attitude and drive that have kept us on the track of continuous improvement in the past twenty years. Therefore, while we take pride in receiving the Inviting School Award, we also remind ourselves that we are only at the beginning of our journey. We are sure that there is still a lot we can learn and do in the years to come.

Note

[1] Staff members in the school are requested to join functional teams in the school according to their preferences. These functional groups include the Counseling Team, Discipline Team, Curriculum Development Team, IT Team, Extra-Curricular Activities Development Team, and the team for Parents Liaisons, etc.

Chapter 11

Building the School
as a Caring
and Collaborative Community:
Hong Kong Experience

Priscilla Lee and Wendy Ho

The way gives them life;
Virtue rears them;
Things give them shape;
Circumstances bring them to maturity.
Therefore the myriad creatures all revere the way
and honor virtue.
Yet the way is revered and virtue honored not because this
is decreed by authority
but because it is natural for them to be treated so.
                              —Lao Tsu: Tao Te Ching
                              (Translated by D.C. Lau)

The Little Dragon from China

A few hundred years ago, Hong Kong was a small fishing village at the Pearl River Delta in southern China. It got its name "Fragrant Harbor" from its manufacture of joss sticks (*pronounced the same as 'Fragrant' in Chinese*) which were largely sent to China in old barges. Today, Hong Kong has emerged as a world-class city after

100 years of British rule. It is now a metropolis with interesting intertwines of the new and the old and a meeting place of the East and the West. Few cities have acquired such dynamism and uniqueness of character because this is where the Chinese heritage still takes its roots while Westernization inevitably sets in.

Being one of the "Four Little Dragons" of Asia, Hong Kong is desperately trying to find its place in a world that is moving fast towards globalization. It is trying to maintain its competitiveness and uniqueness while the other "Little Dragons" are facing the same dilemmas of cultural identity and change. Where is Hong Kong going? This question is asked by educators and policy-makers on the threshold of the *Education Reform*, which sets out to review the Education System and find answers to questions that have long been forgotten.

Growing up with Invitation

With the coming of the *Year of the Dog* according to Chinese almanacs, Hong Kong schools are confronted with the challenges of the *Education Reform* as well as the lingering effects of the economic turmoil in Asia and the world. When unemployment rate soars and stock index plunges, more and more families are on the brink of disintegration. At this time of crisis, schools could fulfill their functions by equipping young people for future challenges and providing them with a safe and happy place for pleasurable learning.

Children growing up with an inviting ambiance can take charge of their life and exert positive influence on those around them. The world would be so much the better if everyone plays a part in making it more inviting. An inviting child often starts with an inviting school.

The Change of Management

Homantin Government Secondary School (HGSS) witnessed a complete change of its Management Team in September 2001 after the retirement of its former Principal, Mrs. Lillian Chan, who led the school along the award-winning path of invitational education years ago. HGSS would not have got that far without her foresight and leadership.

The new Management Team was fortuitous at the time the *Education Reform* was in full momentum and cries for social changes were rampant. Fortunately for the school, the new Team has turned out to have excellent teamwork, shared vision and a commitment to invitational education along the footpath of their predecessor. Looking back to the past year, the school has made strenuous efforts in creating a caring culture through community services and other programs, which signifies that the sustenance of invitational education has been elevated to a higher level. In HGSS, the idea of being "Inviting" has somewhat become a way of life, which, like breathing, just comes naturally without our being aware of it.

To us, the four elements of *Trust, Respect, Optimism,* and *Intentionality* are not merely the products of massive Staff Development Programs. They are continuous efforts in building, lubricating, and repairing relationships. In a profession that deals largely with people, failure to recognize the complexities of human relationships is to miss an important link in effective school management.

I am happy to share with you how we have infiltrated the *Four Elements* in the 5 P's in order to realize the broad ideals of *Invitational Education.*

The Five Ps in HGSS

People

1. Teachers Who Care

The success of Homantin Government Secondary School is the result of the synergic effort of all the people at school. The morale of both staff and students is very high. My two capable Assistant Principals always put forward sound proposals and we form a strong and cohesive Management Team. Teachers are eager to equip themselves with the current trends of education through attending seminars/workshops/training courses in spite of their busy work. They are also willing to have peer lesson observation and share teaching resources.

In a harmonious school environment, our staff collaborates conscientiously towards creating a positive school ethos. Let me cite two incidents to illustrate the atmosphere of our school:

◆ On Teachers' Day held on September 10, 2001, many students made thank you cards and paper flowers for the teachers. There was a song dedication and a friendly football match between teachers and students to celebrate the occasion. A Hong Kong newspaper reporter captured a touching moment when a Grade 11 student presented tokens of thanks to two teachers because he was moved by the act of love they showed the day before. One of the teachers had helped him in the rain when he dashed out in fury after an argument with his girlfriend.

◆ The mother of a Grade 7 student called in despair and expressed her intention to commit suicide. The class teacher kept her on the phone for 45 minutes while two counseling teachers and the school social worker accompanied the student home immediately. The school alerted the police in no time and resolved the crisis after more than 2 hours of professional counseling by teachers. Such excellent teamwork and alertness in responding to contingencies were most commendable.

◆ I am very proud of my staff and students who show dedication and commitment in their respective roles. They provide the very impetus for the school to make big strides in professional and academic development. Here are some examples:

Invitational Sampler:

◆ In the past school year, five more teachers and two janitor staff received Good Customer Service Awards from the Education Department of Hong Kong. (See Appendix 1)

◆ Teachers are dedicated. They come back to school during holidays for extra lessons, running programs, watering flowers and preparing for lessons. Their conscientiousness is very much appreciated.

◆ Students love to stay behind after school to chat, study, play sport, or have barbecue in the serene garden.

◆ There has been a marked increase in the number of students enrolling in community service programs. More than 50% of them participate in voluntary work; some of them have a remarkable record of over 100 service hours.

◆ There is a high level of participation from students, teachers and parents in policy formulation and decision-making. Their views are equally valued.

2. Parental Participation and Support

Parents are important assets of the school. They show support by assisting in various school activities.

Invitational Sampler:

◆ Parents contributed to the large-scale community service program to serve the elderly who live alone. Other than the liaison and planning work, they helped to prepare souvenirs and food for them.

◆ Parents helped organize a two-day Cultural Visit to China at Christmas.

◆ A parent gave a talk on China's Entry to WTO and Biotechnology.

◆ A parent skilful at handicraft volunteered to teach students to make souvenirs for guests.

◆ Parents took part in the adjudication of student projects.

◆ Parents showed support by offering to conduct mock interviews for our students at their work place.

◆ Parents made generous donations of scholarships.

3. Support from Alumnae

Past students show a strong sense of belonging to the school. The love and attachment they have for their alma mater certainly helps to boost morale and strengthen ties.

Invitational Sampler:

◆ To enhance the school environment, the alumnae donated money to build a green house in our school garden. It is a pride for HGSS.

◆ With donations from alumnae, all classrooms are air-conditioned.

◆ They donate scholarships to recognize outstanding achievement.

◆ They organized a reunion camp and gave free places to current students.

◆ They organized ball games and other activities in order to strengthen ties with the school.

◆ They gave talks at school as a form of motivation and encouragement.

Policies

School policies are reviewed and modified to align with the spirit of *Invitational Education*. They can be reflected in the following ways:

◆ The opening hours of the school are extended to enable students to stay behind for revision or recreational activities.

◆ School Discipline is to be taken as positive measures to facilitate personal development. As a result, the lengthy school regulations are simplified to eight lines of positive behavior expected of students. The wordings have also been changed to convey a positive message.

◆ An *Atonement System* is adopted in relation to minor

offences to give students motivating drive to learn from their mistakes.

◆ Similarly, a *Student Award Scheme* is launched to nurture desirable behavior and consolidate self-discipline.

◆ A *School Self-Evaluation* on student achievement and school improvement was conducted to determine the priorities for the coming school year.

◆ Through *Student Self-Evaluation,* students were given the chance to reflect on their learning attitude, strategies and outcome. In the evaluation form, they could also give suggestions to teachers on ways to help them improve. This was built on mutual trust.

◆ Students are given ample opportunities to take charge of important occasions so as to broaden their exposure and boost their confidence. For example, they are asked to give short talks and do presentations at assemblies. They also act as MC's at school functions.

Programs

"Love and Care" was the central theme for the past school year. A lot of programs were designed around this theme. They include:

Invitational Sampler:

◆ The Principal and teachers delivered inspiring speeches on *"Weekly Quotes"* in the morning.

◆ Students designed "Good Wish Cards" and sent them to their parents and grandparents to show appreciation.

◆ Students showed appreciation to teachers on Teachers' Day.

◆ Christmas celebrations under the theme of "Love and Peace." Events included a singing contest, a cookery competition and a bulletin board design competition. Response was excellent.

◆ There was a "Caring Ambassadors Scheme" and a "Community Service Group" to promote student voluntary service. Students looked after sick children, old people and handicapped people. They have earned a very good reputation in the district because of their willingness to serve.

◆ Senior form students offer help and guidance to lower form students by serving as Peer Counselors.

◆ Even lower form students could learn to serve by conducting after school activity sessions in Hunghom Government Primary School.

◆ Umbrellas, clean school uniforms and towels were on loan to students at wet weather.

Our school places great importance on *Teaching and Learning.* A series of programs were conducted to enhance teaching effectiveness:

Invitational Sampler:

◆ To develop students' generic skills, we made it the highlight of the year to promote Project-based Learning. Students' work was displayed on a Student Project Display Day in March. It was a great success.

◆ To cater for learner differences, we offer enrichment programs for able students and remedial classes for the less able ones.

◆ To raise the standard of English, overseas eye-opener programs and supportive programs were arranged. There were study trips to Thailand, New Zealand and England.

◆ To enhance the leadership of students, they were chosen to represent the school in open forums, language committee meetings, cultural visits and interviews hosted by leading government officials or legislators.

◆ Our school has joined the IQEA (Improving the Quality of Education for All) Project organized jointly by the

Education Department and the University of Nottingham in an effort to enhance teaching effectiveness.

◆ Teachers employed student-focused strategies to motivate students to learn and sustain their interest in learning.

The development of Collaborative Culture was also one of the Major Concerns in the previous school year. It was achieved through the following programs:

Invitation Sampler:

◆ The message of creating a *Collaborative Culture* at school was conveyed very clearly to the whole school at the beginning of the term.

◆ To promote professional development, teachers were asked to open their classes for peer observation and conduct debriefing sessions afterwards.

◆ Heads of subject departments were encouraged to pool together their teaching resources and set up a data bank for common use.

◆ The school timetable was readjusted to allow time for professional sharing and collaborative lesson planning.

◆ Staff Development Workshops were conducted by renowned experts in *Collaborative Learning* to encourage teachers to make use of such skills in their classrooms.

◆ Teachers were encouraged to make better use of community resources to support their teaching. Help had been sought from youth centers, religious groups and Universities.

◆ An English Foundation School in the district was asked to conduct English Activity Programs for our students. The working relationship was to be continued in the next school year.

◆ The active promotion of Project-based Learning is a good example of *Collaborative Learning.*

◆ Parents worked in collaboration with teachers in major school functions such as a Tree Planting Day, a visit to China, Sports Day and mock interviews.

◆ Several Joint School Oral Practice Sessions were arranged jointly with more than 10 schools in the neighborhood. Student response was most enthusiastic.

Processes

Our school policies are clear, transparent, and student-centered. They are clearly written in the School Policy and Procedure Manual. The opinions of all stakeholders are solicited in the formulation of policies; which are reviewed systematically through informal discussions, formal staff meetings, committee meetings, Parent-Teacher Association meetings and questionnaires. For example, the views of teachers and students were collected and used as the basis for the formulation of the Major Concerns for the next school year.

Invitational Sampler:

◆ Good teamwork is the key to any effective management. Our Assistant Principals took the lead in sharing their teaching resources and opening their classes for peer observation.

◆ The senior management set a role model by showing respect to all staff regardless of their status and ranks.

◆ Open channels for communication are provided. For example, on a Staff Development Day, teachers were asked to discuss in groups and reflect on such issues as ways to alleviate their workload and areas for school improvement.

◆ The senior management responded promptly to staff suggestions. For example, work procedures were streamlined and extra clerical workers employed to provide support and enhance efficiency.

◆ To enhance learning effectiveness, a school self-evaluation was conducted on Student Achievement. Students were asked to reflect, evaluate and assess their performance in learning after the mid-year examination. Teachers were also asked to evaluate their learning effectiveness and all-round development through discussions.

◆Appreciation and praise were given promptly in recognition for good performance.

◆ The views of parents, students and teachers were solicited in:

> drafting the Annual School Plan for the coming year;
> changing the design of girls' summer uniform;
> amending the school rule regarding the wearing of school badges;
> allowing students to bring mobile phones to school.

Students could design their own class rules and mottos.

Places

Our school campus is obviously an inviting one. Situated in a quiet residential area, it draws admiration with its beautiful green house and tennis court; a blessing not found in any other government or aided schools. Guests and parents invariably marvel at the blooming orchids in the green house. Students enjoy reading under the shade of Banyan trees and having barbecue in the back yard of the school garden.

We have also received an Outstanding Green School Award-Merit Prize this year. Our school is one of the few schools in Hong Kong possessing valuable specimens of endangered species (a crocodile, a hawksbill, a water monitor and a green sea turtle) donated by the Agriculture, Fisheries and Conservation Department. We displayed these specimens in March 2002 to draw people's attention to environmental protection and their appreciation of the beauty of Nature.

As with all Inviting Schools, visitors are greeted warmly at the counter by our minor staff. The electronic notice board also displays welcome signs and important notices of the day. Teachers are informed immediately through the PA system in response to parents and visitors.

We purposely post different Chinese and English famous quotes near the main staircase to motivate students to learn. To promote information technology, multimedia projectors and computer units were installed in all classrooms last year.

The senior management is eager to improve the school environment. Renovation work undertaken in the past two years include:

Invitational Sampler:

◆ Air-conditioning the School Hall and all the classrooms.

◆ Lighting at school was improved.

◆ The General Office was fully renovated to appear much more inviting.

◆ Multi-media projectors and computers were installed in all classrooms.

◆ Defective blackboards, bulletin board, lockers and doors were replaced.

◆ Safety nets were fixed at main staircases.

◆ Replacement of windows.

◆ Renovation of 5 storerooms.

◆ Purchase of 40 storage cabinets to make the place look tidier.

◆ Drinking fountains were installed at various places for student use.

◆ The ventilation and flushing system of all toilets were improved.

◆ More storage space was created for staff and students.

The staff of Homantin Government Secondary School are proud of being recognized as an inviting school and are keen to ensure that we remain as such. It is also our conviction to put children first and make relentless effort to enhance the effectiveness of teaching and learning. With a staff of highly committed teachers, Homantin Government Secondary School will continue to grow from strength to strength and be totally committed to invitational education.

Chapter 12

Becoming Intentionally Inviting:
A Case Study in Independent
South African Schools

Nicky Aylmer, Di Dawes, and Martyn van der Merwe

Introduction

South African schools are consistently challenged to provide excellent education and opportunities for all learners in the post-Apartheid era. However, amidst the ongoing political and social adjustments in the country and in the region, as well as unsatisfactory national examination results in the past, this seems to be increasingly difficult task. Many parents and educators are placing their trust in the independent school system as a possible foil to combat these challenges. A common perception held is that education in so-called 'private' schools is superior to that in the fully state-subsidized schools. This perception is based on the assumption that independent schools can deliver more adequate and better facilities and opportunities, that these schools attract 'better' and possibly more-qualified educators, that these schools can supply an ethos, and 'old-boys' culture and network which may lead to better employment opportunities.

Irrespective of these perceptions, it remains clear that now, more than ever, a theory of practice which will address pertinent issues at the root in education in South Africa, is required. The invitational education model could well provide a framework within which to act in an educationally acceptable manner in any educative context. In this chapter, a comparative view of two independent schools will be given, endeavoring to determine to what extent invitational education is being practiced, to highlight possible problem areas and to suggest possible solutions using the tenets of invitational education.

We further claim that the ethos and practices in the two independent schools observed are 'unknowingly' or unintentionally inviting. The ethos and practices of both schools will be observed, described and compared from the perspective of two teachers respectively teaching at each of the schools. These observations were made during the semester that the two mentioned students were studying a course in invitational education as part of their graduate program. It was therefore, their observations from a 'limited' perspective, as they had not been reading and applying the theory for a lengthy period of time.

The descriptions will focus on the extent to which invitational education offers possible practical solutions to specific problems centering on the five P's (people, places, policies, programs, and practices) as the areas of application of the invitational model. The authors believe that perhaps the greatest challenge for the teachers at these schools is to move from being unintentionally inviting to becoming intentionally inviting. Guidelines applicable to this specific context and the challenge to be intentionally inviting will be suggested.

Mandy's School

During our studies of invitational education we were constantly made aware of the need to create more inviting schools. In our context in South Africa, we are attempting to be more outcomes-based in our approach to learning and development, we are endeavoring to be more inclusive in our policies and practices and are attempting to become a 'working' democracy, also at school level. I was beginning to wonder about the invitational quality of our school and was confronted with a number of questions about the school. Could our school really be regarded as an invitational? If so, what factors contributed to the school that has integrated invitational education?

Do people, especially teachers at the school who are not familiar with the theory of invitational education, instinctively implement some aspects of the approach? If indeed they do, the question that remains unanswered is, "Why?"

The basic principles of invitational theory were adhered to in this observation and enquiry and the five P's (people, places, policies, programs and processes) were used as the basic units for assessing the invitational quality of this school. Accordingly, the school and its practices will be discussed according to this framework.

The History/Background
of the School Based on the Five P's

Process

The school is based on a Christian ethos. It was opened in 1997 as the realization of a vision and dream of three, then Superintendents of education, in management positions in the Department of Education. These men made it their mission to move from the paradigm of 'government employees' to 'successful businessmen'. This mission statement should seriously be challenged in terms of the Christian ethos which was marketed to potential 'clients' of this 'Inviting' school.

By basing the school on a Christian ethos, the aim was to instill traditional Christian values and principles in the school and the learners. Unfortunately, this ethos, in partnership with prohibitive private school fees, could be viewed as disinviting by certain members of the community. Of interest is the fact that certain of the pioneer parents were not of the Christian faith. Their reasons for selecting the schools were that they wanted what they perceived as "right" for their children. 'Right' would equate to quality education, good results, excellent facilities and opportunities. One could argue whether such expectations are necessarily authentically 'inviting'. On the surface level most potential parents would see this school as having the 'inviting' recipe for them. This 'recipe' also suited many of the incoming staff members who also enrolled their own children, with confidence, in the school.

The initial goal was to start a school with small classes, learner-teacher ratio was becoming a concern in the restructuring of education in a democratic South Africa, and excellent teachers. This coupled with the Christian ethos appealed to many parents and before the second year of its existence the school had doubled in number of learners. It was aspects such as the aforementioned, which 'attracted' parents and teachers and can be seen to be 'inviting' although not intentionally implemented.

The school consists of a preparatory school and a secondary school. Both the principals of the preparatory and the secondary schools have shown a remarkable ability to select like-minded people when appointing staff. Those that have been appointed are very talented, well qualified and hardworking. In addition, they are said to be committed Christians. In practice, this has led to a staff contingent who are known to be compassionate and kind as well as educators who are indeed willing to make tremendous sacrifices for their school and its learners. This innate 'ability to care and respect others' was further supported by the relief many of the teachers no doubt felt at moving form the 'arena of government education', which was rapidly changing, to schooling in the private sector where change was experienced as growth rather than frustration. The teachers were quite content to be expected to 'go the extra mile.'

While many of these values and principles described are essentially inviting, the ways in which they are modeled and practiced can be regarded as being 'disinviting.' For example, many of the teachers come from a Christian background. The Christian faith relies on compassion, respect and love for the fellowman, obedience and even sacrifice. These values, although fairly conservative in nature, could well indicate an 'intuitive and unintentional' inviting attitude. This value system necessitates a view on discipline and responsibility as being a priority. This may, in turn, lead to a strict code of conduct being adhered to with possibly a system of punishment in place and may even be enforced in some cases. These values and the policies and procedures developed from them may therefore be interpreted as 'one of control' and may be experienced as disinviting by those involved. Within the changing South African context, this more prescriptive and controlled environment could be experienced as more secure and even less stressful and would be believed to 'inviting' by the educators involved, whilst perceived as disinviting by others.

Against the backdrop of the initial vision of the 'founders,' the initial responsibility was not only on the educative activities of teaching and learning but rather to use these and other related activities to market the school as a successful, growing concern. This, unfortunately, created one of the lesser inviting qualities of the school, namely pressure on the school (inclusive of all concerned) to perform and to be viewed as a growing enterprise. The intended recipients of the 'a unintentional invitation' to join a small, intimate, caring school based on Christian principles, became disillusioned at the realization of the school now fast becoming a vast, busy, pressurized environment which had to keep this momentum going from one year to the next. It meant that the initial 'intended' invitation had become 'unintentionally' disinviting. Testimony to this, is the observation that of the seventeen staff members who originally committed themselves to this school, only five remain. It can perhaps be assumed that the original message sent to invite staff to pioneer the school is no longer in existence and has unintentionally placed extreme pressure on the staff and learners.

For those educators who had started teaching with the inception of the school, this stress, although self-inflicted, was greater than they had anticipated. The school's message of achievement attracts a certain type of parent and learner. Parents normally attracted to the school want results and the learners seek recognition. People, who do not find this kind of striving invigorating but rather daunting, experience this situation as a disinviting one.

The school is an 'inclusive' school in theory with no excluding entrance criteria. The fact that the school is run on the principles of an 'enterprise' will likely exclude a number of learners on financial grounds. The fact that there are not any specific entrance criteria may be experienced as inviting, but due to the nature of the school in terms of the expected performances of learners by parents and teachers, learners who do not meet with the high expectations may experience disinviting scenarios. Learners are unavoidably made aware of their lack of achievement in terms of the school's ethos regarding academic excellence and invariably feel disinvited and in many cases the impact on the self-perceptions of learners are negative. The context of abundant financial support creates a spirit of competition amongst learners. Those learners whose parents believe in the ethos and values embodied in the school and its staff and who are generally making huge financial sacrifices to enroll their children at the school, may feel disinvited as the may find the comparison of assets amongst learners as very demeaning in the spirit of competition.

This also affects the staff members to the extent that the parents of the majority of learners from privileged backgrounds paying high school fees, lay claim to the right of actually having a say in how the staff should be going about their professional task. In essence, within a democratic context, this is indeed part of the process, but teachers' professional status and esteem needs to be acknowledged as well. Collaborate, yes; dictate NO!

Place

It has taken five years for the school to become established. The building is now complete. The campus consists of a pre-primary school, a preparatory school and a secondary school. The entire complex is very pleasing to the eye. Although there are no large trees and well-established gardens yet, the grounds are neatly kept. Security measures allowing access to the buildings during and after school hours are also in place.

The buildings have been designed on European lines, a single story built around central corridors. These are wide, airy and spacious. Garden atriums act as walkways between classes. The learners can move quickly and quietly to the next class. There are no staircases other than those leading to the administrative block. This is ideal for learners with physical barriers to learning. Sports facilities are excellent with virtually all needs are catered for. As sport is very close to the preparatory school principal's heart, little has been spared in the establishment of sports fields, tennis courts and a swimming pool.In addition to this, the great hall is ideal for hosting a full junior and senior choir. There is also a large stage that can be utilized by an active drama group.

There are carports for the staff members' motor vehicles. Parking for parents, however, is minimal and may be experienced as disinviting. Despite the fact that the arrival and departure times of the respective schools are staggered, the limited parking space invariably leads to congestion.

People and Policies

As stated earlier, since the inception of the school, teachers who have applied at the school have generally been of excellent quality and have often moved from a promotional post to a lower post level to become part of this school. It therefore goes without saying that the staff contingent is seen as a tremendous resource pool. Teaching styles and approaches within the school is therefore varied. The best of policies have been refined and implemented. Teachers with many years of experience have 'married together' various policies administrative programs. Ideas that work have been put into practice. Those ideas that do not work, have been abandoned.

The staff regards respect as paramount, thus creating an 'un-intentionally' inviting teacher stance. Learners are valued. Holistic education is offered ensuring that each learner is allowed the opportunity to excel. There is a relationship of trust and open communication is encouraged, although this is carefully monitored. The staff believes in their learners and is dedicated to their progress. They are committed thereby being intentional in the educative process. I doing this the staff enact the basic tenets of invitational education.

The policies and activities at the school are guided by the principles of character education, which in turn is supported by the Christian ethos. Children are taught that age old traditional values such as integrity, loyalty, and good work ethic are the foundations upon which they should base their lives. Yet, there are ample opportunities created for learners to form their own opinions on issues.

There is an underlying competitiveness between staff members, possibly created by the type of individuals working at the school. The staff is largely self-starters who take the initiative and are not afraid to bring years of expertise to the endeavor. Management has seen fit to give each staff member a specific portfolio containing basic instructions, which is then left up to the initiative and drive of the staff member. The staff, being self-motivated individuals, carries out these instructions to the best of their ability. They do, however, expect recognition. One could reason that the agendas created by this policy are not overt and could lead to a number of hidden and unhealthy agendas developing. These agendas create challenges and the staff readily accepts the challenges. The problem facing the principal with such a high-powered staff is to give each one the recognition that he/she deserves or thinks he/she deserves! The experience of this recognition has had the effect that it was not perceived to be adequate and therefore not inviting. A number of instances have occurred where staff has become very demotivated.

The curriculum is broad-based. The school attempts combines the Outcome-Based Education (OBE) approach with the very formalized 'traditional' activities associated with the ethos of the school, namely Religious education, Bible education, daily devotions and assemblies. OBE relies to an extent on group work and collaboration in the learning situation. Unfortunately group work takes place to a lesser degree in most classes. Although assessment is ongoing and continual, formal examinations are still being written in the senior phases. This form of assessment is stressful for the younger learners and although it is a life-skill to be mastered, examinations are not seen as invitational by parents, learners and the staff. The staff, therefore, tries their best to downplay the importance of examinations by stating that it is merely part of the learning process.

Discipline policies as may be expected, are rather prescriptive and even punitive at times. This may be due to the ethos of the school and seem to contradict the general tone of 'invitationality' of the school. Discipline policies are very 'traditionally' oriented. Unacceptable behavior is not tolerated and admonished. A high percentage of the staff are male teachers however, there are few discipline problems. On the positive side, although the tone of the policies is very directive and strict, correct behavior is modeled and modified. Policies regarding the admonishing of learners are related to the general ethos of the school. There is a detention policy in place that is seldom utilized. The focus of these 'after-school detention' sessions is rather on identifying learners who need support and stay for supervised homework on a daily basis. Community service may also be required of learners in the secondary school who transgress. For certain parents this may appear disinviting. The majority of them, however, voiced gratitude for the boundaries and parameters placed upon their children.

Programs

With the emphasis on the eight new learning areas of the curriculum in South African schools, as well as the focus on becoming more skilled to participate in the world of work and citizenship, the school is administering an excellent life-skills program under the leadership of a registered educational psychologist. These program aims at equipping learners with the necessary study skills, career and future orientation skills, social skills and sex education programs. In our country with its plethora of social and economic deficits, these skills are of absolute necessity.

Academic remediation is offered at the school during and after hours. This has an assisted learning structure and runs in conjunction with, and in addition to, classroom teaching. Once again the staff that are involved with the remedial program are highly qualified and experienced. As the school endeavors to cater for holistic development of learners, a full music program is also offered, both intra- and extra-curricular. Learners are exposed to a vast range of musical instruments. Opportunities to play these at assemblies and various other ceremonies are created. The staff involved in this area of teaching all has degrees in Music.

Parental and community involvement are a priority at the school. Parents have always been welcome at the school and invited to participate. Many have been with the school since inception and regard the school as a part of their family. They are involved in developing the gardens, flower arrangements and organization of functions, drama groups, photography and extra-mural assistance. Some parents offer their services in covering learners' books (proceeds going to the school coffers) and transporting learners to all kinds of functions and activities at no cost.

Over the duration of weekends, the school is a forum for lectures and presentations as part of the Whole-school development approach expected of schools. There is a French lesson group that meets weekly and an ADHD workshop is held monthly. The great hall and other venues are used for various functions. In the spirit of giving there are community outreach programs to disadvantaged schools and societies for the needy. Visits to nearby old age homes and hospitals are a regular occurrence inline with the Christian ethos of the school. Caring for the larger community is encouraged through ongoing collections of food and clothing for the homeless and the needy.

Conclusion

The view portrayed of my school, may be considered to have some invitational qualities as well as some that are less inviting. As a member of the teaching staff at the school, I wondered about how we, as the important cogs in the wheels of this school, perceived the school. I was secondly intrigued by the possibility that many of the members of staff were 'doing the inviting things' without realizing.

Were they, even though they were not familiar with the theory of invitational education, instinctively implementing some aspects of the approach? Possible answers to this question may be:

◆ That the environment is a controlled one and that some of the staff is of a conforming nature.

◆ That the "like-minded" religious ethos that underlies the attitudes, approaches towards and treatment of the learners, in this case a Christian ethos, was similar to some of the tenets of the invitational approach.

◆ That many of the staff members have their own children enrolled in the school therefore creating a doubly loyalty situation.

Jana Describes Her School

The mission statement of the school in which I work is an inviting one. The school is described as a "progressive, co-educational, non-denominational and non-racial (institution) committed to preparing young people to meet the challenges of the future." It endeavors to do this by creating a vibrant, stimulating and enjoyable environment in which students are taught to think independently, understand content and apply it to various situations.

Our statement of purpose further suggests that we will look for excellence in all our students, at the same time as deliberately encouraging co-operation rather than competition. It asserts that each student has a talent to be discovered and developed. Learning is best achieved, according to our ethos, when it is an exciting and enjoyable process and not a source of anxiety and despair. Teachers, who will inspire, enthuse and encourage students to reach their potential and maximize their ability, are thus selected. With this in mind a stimulating, warm, caring and challenging classroom atmosphere is expected.

The aim is to implement a caring, empathetic school policy that respects the needs of each individual as well as their dignity and rights. Students, according to our mission statement, will be made to feel that they have a significant contribution to make and they will be encouraged to develop sensitivity towards the needs, strengths and weaknesses of others. Our end goal is to have open-minded, responsible, balanced individuals, resilient in adversity and capable of caring relationships, leave our school.

The policy of the school is clearly defined but it is my contention that in order to achieve what we set out to do we need to move from being unintentionally inviting to intentionally inviting. The reason for this is that inconsistency is damaging as it breeds discontent and suspicion. I aim to give a brief overview of the History of the school to date and to highlight areas which should be addressed so that we can adopt an intentionally inviting stance.

Overview

At this stage, six years down the line, there are six Primary schools, five High schools, two Universities and a number of Pre-primary schools under the same umbrella. The school in which I am involved is dynamic. The staff room and reception area buzz with activity from early morning to late afternoon. Most of the staff arrives at school between half and three quarters of an hour before classes begin. It is a time to share breakfast, a huge mug of percolated coffee and a good laugh. Our staff seems to laugh loudly and often. We also cry at times and have some heated discussions during meetings. The platform is open and people are able to express what they think and feel freely. It can be uncomfortable at times but it makes work interesting, it is a challenge and each member of staff has an equal voice.

A high school science teacher, with a vision, and a mum with some business background, started the school. The vision was to see students develop to their full potential as individuals and to provide an education without fear in which both teachers and students would be treated with dignity and respect. At that stage there was a gap in the market. The education provided by Government schools in our area was good, there were many successful Private schools, Special education needs were catered for and there were Remedial schools for students with learning difficulties. There were however, few schools specifically for the average to the above average pupil. Thus the school, aiming at the average to above average pupil was born. It started as a high school, which ran for four years and produced excellent results both on the sports field and in the classroom.

The idea was not to be elitist but to reach, as far as possible, a niche market and then address issues pertinent to that group. The perception was that schools, which try to cater for the general population usually, end up focussing on problems experienced by the slower learner because of their urgency. Then, due to political change in the country, Government schools had to face the prospect of very large classes, teacher morale seemed to be at its lowest ebb and the curriculum was about to be changed altogether. This was not a problem itself, the issue was that few teachers understood the approach which was to be adopted and the training programs provided were not sufficient to instill confidence. Many people began to look for alternatives to State education.

Our school expanded and a Pre-primary and Primary school were opened. Later, due to its success, other schools came under the same umbrella. Some were taken over by our organization and others were built. The policy was to have the "best" teachers involved with subjects about whom they were passionate, small classes, twenty-five being the maximum and students who were both able and prepared to take responsibility for their own learning. This would best be achieved, they believed and as invitational education asserts, in a relaxed, informal and beautiful environment.

Our buildings are modern with wide corridors, open spaces and light and airy classrooms. On entering the reception area many people comment on its almost "hotel like" quality and atmosphere. Fresh flowers add the finishing touches to a building designed with care. Our gardens and fields are well tended. We have some large trees and have planted others, which will give good shade in a few years time. There is no institutional feel. Classrooms seldom look the same from one day to the next. Single square desks are arranged according to the type of lesson and the involvement required by the students for the task at hand. Desks may be grouped for easy discussion or they may be placed in formal rows when skill acquisition is the focus.

Because our teachers are expected to and trusted to perform, there are no "checking up" procedures as such. We are encouraged to explore different methods and approaches in the classroom and teachers are given room to experiment with new ideas. It is very easy, however, to slip back into the "tried and tested" ways of achieving ones end. For this reason I would suggest that we, as colleagues, continue to make time to share our ideas and experiences with each other in order to keep the education which we provide, fresh and vibrant. The problem is that teachers have to be confident within them selves or fierce and unnecessary competition can result.

It is our contention that the first five minutes of each lesson will determine the response and level of interest that we can expect from the students. If students are disruptive our initial questions should be directed towards the atmosphere in the classroom. Was the teacher sufficiently prepared? Were there unnecessary interruptions? Was too much time spent on organizational matters and if so are there more efficient ways to go about it? Was the lesson boring? Were the students encouraged to be actively involved in their learning?

For the first few years, while the labour laws of the country allowed it, all the teachers employed were "head hunted". They were selected according to the subject need of the school and the reputed performance of the teachers. We consequently have a dynamic, strong and enthusiastic staff. It has been our experience, however, that even though some teachers were good at understanding and implementing a system, such as that used in Government schools, they were not able to adapt to our system which is innovative and different and requires educators as opposed to teachers for its implementation. The lack of specific guidance caused serious concern for many teachers. We also found that other schools, particularly independent schools, were angered by the "head hunting" policy which they referred to as "poaching," and it has taken many years to begin to heal the rift which resulted. We have had to recognize that independence is not achieved without some form of interdependence. It also became apparent that in most schools, there tend to be one or two leaders and the rest of the staff are fairly happy to comply with the decisions made by good management. We have a number of teachers who were in leadership positions in other schools. This has created some difficulties with the dynamics of the staff as historically we are used to an authoritarian structure of management. In order to become more democratic it would serve us well to learn to verbalize and justify our point of view and listen actively to each other, these are tenets of invitational education.

Our school has a flat structure of authority in which every member is both expected to and required to take ownership of their particular area involvement and the problems that they encounter. Even though this sounds inviting in practice it can prove to be very frustrating. There is no accountability and the tendency to blame shift is apparent. It is also difficult to know what one can and can't do without "stepping on the toes" of ones colleagues.

In the process of working out how best to meet our staffing needs we initially had a large turnover but this seems to have settled over the past few years. Staff meetings become a platform for discussion and issues are looked at from as many different angles as possible, with a view to provide the best education for our students. We do, however, still have to learn not to be sidetracked by secondary issues that frustrate the process of reaching viable solutions. Our aim is to develop a working relationship that is characterized by a shared sense of purpose, mutual respect and a willingness to negotiate. This implies a sharing of information, responsibilities, skills, decision-making and accountability. This is an inviting stance but in order to become intentionally inviting policies should be reviewed constantly and an attempt to vary our programs should be made so that we stay on the cutting edge of education. Even though it gives security, the tendency to turn principles into fixed practices can detract from being relevant in a rapidly changing society. Our statement of purpose suggests that policies will be reviewed constantly but in practice it is time consuming and takes commitment to implement.

Once a year our teachers are invited to participate in an appraisal with the head. The procedure is as follows. Each teacher grades his or her self, on a scale of 1-9 in specific, well defined areas of performance. A meeting is then held with the head and, after discussion, a joint rating is marked on the same form in a different colour. Discussion is frank and open. At the conclusion of the exercise the teacher, with input from the head, indicates goals for the following year, which are then written down in order of priority. This exercise not only provides an opportunity for head and teacher to discuss concerns and vision for the future, but it is also an important tool used to determine the type of increase, within certain parameters, given to each teacher. It is the only form of teacher evaluation within our system. South African teachers are used to having much stricter controlling measures. This method fits the tenants of invitational education in that it is designed to be a "doing with" exercise, it encourages mutual respect between the head and the teacher, it demands accountability, facilitates negotiation and provides a vehicle for an individual's strengths and dreams to be challenged into future action.

One of the most important principles of our school is to give the students an opportunity to develop as individuals. With this in mind, a "multi form" as opposed to a uniform has been designed. It consists of a number of items of clothing that can be worn to give a different yet uniform look. For example the girls may decide to wear a pinafore, a skirt, shorts or long trousers along with a T-shirt or a golf shirt. We have thus given the students a choice, recognizing their need for some sense of control, within a set of clearly defined specifics. As a consequence we have very few weird and wonderful adaptations to the uniform. Prior to introducing the "multi form" a questionnaire regarding uniforms was completed by 500 teenagers in our area. They were asked to indicate if they would prefer to wear "civvies," a multiform or a uniform. The majority liked the idea of the multiform.

Our aim is to educate, rather than 'school' students, which is why we provide a more varied curriculum to that which is currently available in other schools in South Africa. By law each pupil is required to have one of our thirteen official languages as a medium of instruction and one other as a second language. We also offer a third language, French, Greek, German (in some schools) or Hebrew, at Primary school level should students choose to study in that direction. Every pupil is required to do music, art, drama, computer studies, technology education and either physical education or ballet until Grade 7. Specialist teachers are responsible for these subjects. Each pupil is also required to attend Moral, Bible, or Jewish Studies classes. The same life skill is taught concurrently in each lesson across the grade, but the approach is different. Bible and Jewish Studies classes have a religious element to the lessons. The program we are planning to introduce, at Primary school level, focuses on the development of a strong and positive concept of self as well as the building of character.

One of the important skills mentioned in invitational education is that of assertion. It has been our experience that, by the time our students are in the higher grades of Primary school, they all, including the painfully shy, have enough confidence to participate in some form of public speaking. We attribute this to the fact that drama is a core curriculum subject facilitated by specialist and dynamic drama teachers. All of our students are exposed to and participate in various forms of performing arts programs during their Primary school years. Choral verse has been a strong focus. This enables the shy pupil to participate with support.

When there is a change of period students from one class move in various directions depending on their choice of subject. For the first few weeks in Grade 1 the teacher will take students to their next class but after that they move freely from one class to another. Every now and then we have to remind children not to run on the corridors and to move quickly and quietly but on the whole the students seem to respond well to the more relaxed, informal nature of the school. Once in a while a little one may find him or herself "lost" but there is a comfortable relationship between students and staff which means that help is always close at hand. Our corridors and assembly places are a little louder than most South African teachers are used to, but, once a lesson or assembly begins the students are generally quiet and attentive.

It is our policy to praise in public and reprimand in private. No ridicule, sarcasm or embarrassment is tolerated. Teachers are encouraged to respond and not react. We support each other in this regard. We recently introduced an invitational education discipline model of the six C's (concern, confer, consult, confront, combat and conciliate) and have had good results. Having a framework within which to work has enabled us to behave in an intentionally inviting manner more consistently. Students are given the freedom to air their grievances but are required and to show respect for each other and for their teachers. However, the problem is that we assume that students know how to communicate in this manner. I believe that it is our responsibility to demonstrate and to teach them appropriate ways to voice feelings of dissatisfaction and appreciation. This is part of relating and investing.

Students who wish to attend our school are assessed so that, as far as possible, we can be sure that they will benefit from our system. This has produced some misconceptions amongst both the staff and the parents. When students present with difficulties the question often raised by the staff is why they were admitted in the first place. The parents are also very demanding and assume that if the child was admitted to our school they are bright and will therefore not experience any problems with learning. One of the reasons for this perception is that the school has projected an image that suits the High school but not the Primary school. The confusion has come about because of the policy to accept only average to above average students into the school. It is in fact very difficult to ascertain intellectual ability, particularly at a Pre-primary and Junior Primary level. IQ tests may give a rough indication of performance on certain tests but are not used due to the negative connotation associated with the tests in South

Africa as well as the incorrect perceptions created by the results. Our prospective learners at Primary school level are screened for major barriers to learning and development that would best be handled in specialized schools. The High school, however, has an entrance requirement of an aggregate of 60%.

The perceptions discussed put enormous and unrealistic demands on the teacher. In order to combat the situation I suggest that parent information evenings be used to address the concerns of both the teachers and the parent body. If, as is explained in invitational education, perceptions play a large role in our understanding, we need to start talking more in an attempt to understand each other. Education is not something "done" by a school it is an exercise that relies on a partnership between the home, the environment and the school. Once again this is time consuming and positive results are often slow to materialize. It therefore takes determination and perseverance to implement and follow through with a program of this nature. Engaging in listening behaviour should be a reflective activity to facilitate true communication.

In conclusion I would like to suggest that, "where there is no vision, people perish" (Proverbs 29:18). Our mission statement is value driven. I believe that it needs to be brought into focus and discussed often. This is so that the paradigm shift and momentum, which are necessary to effect change, can take place.

Comparison of Mandy's and Jana's Schools

In our comparison we will examine the places, people, policies, programs, and processes of each school.

Place

Both schools are newly developed. They are aesthetically pleasing to the eye and there is a welcoming window into the school through an approachable administrative staff. Nothing has been spared in the financing of intra and extra mural facilities.

People

While our parent body is similar in that they come from a like socio-economic background they differ in the following ways. Mandy's parents are more conservative. They subscribe to traditional Christian values that are reinforced through character education. In Mandy's school the 'richness' of other cultures and diversity may be excluded. Jane's parents, on the other hand, are more "avant garde' tending towards a 'laissez faire' approach. They both, however, have aspirations of the school and exert pressure on both their children and the staff with unreasonable demands at times.

The students at the school differ. Mandy's students tend to conform easily and are used to a strict, disciplined environment. The students do not question the system. In general, the students at Jane's school seem to be more free spirited. The students question and challenge ideas and the system continually. The students come from a varied ethnic and cosmopolitan background. Interestingly enough, neither school has had to contend with many serious discipline issues. At both schools students are encouraged to develop to their full potential, academically, on the sports field, culturally, emotionally and socially. Although students from both schools, according to our perception, are assertive, the learners at Jane's school tend to be more open-minded and liberal and Mandy's less individual and 'more people pleasing.'

Both sets of staff are well qualified, highly competent and hard working, having high expectations of themselves and others. During the five or so years of existence both schools experienced a large turnover of staff. The leadership in Mandy's is of an authoritarian nature and is seldom queried. At the other end of the scale Jane's staff constantly question and challenge policies and procedures, each other, the system and how to achieve their stated goals.

Policies

Even though the policies within Jane's school are fluid there is a structured statement of purpose that has become the reference point when decisions are made. In addition to the mission statement of Mandy's school, like-mindedness ensures that traditional values are the basis of policy decisions.

Programs

Even though the wide selection of programs and subjects within Jane's school appear to be inviting, it is apparent, that for some students the foundational skills required for learning are not given sufficient time for consolidation. School however, is not humdrum or boring. The narrower curriculum of Mandy's school allows for more focus on the basics.

Processes

While the finely tuned systems, which run smoothly and without a hitch at Mandy's school, promote security they can stifle and restrict initiative. In contrast the freedom and lack of structure within Jane's school allows for growth and creativity but it can create confusion and frustration for teachers.

The Challenge

The greatest challenge facing the staff members of both these schools is to move from being unintentionally inviting to becoming intentionally inviting. In order to do this they must be aware that they are behaving in an unintentionally inviting manner. It also needs to be recognized that this stance presents problems in that it is not consistent at this time and as such the teachers do not have a dependable position from which to operate. The staff members realize that they are good teachers but are not aware of the reasons for their successes or failures. The logical suggestion is that the teachers become familiar with and identify with the characteristics which support being intentionally inviting.

One of the most important tenets is that of communicating openly and honestly with each other. This encourages trust and respect to develop between staff and students. It requires sensitivity and an attitude of "doing with" rather than "doing to." The teacher's perception should be one of optimism in that they believe in the abilities of their students. This enhances a positive self -concept. Teachers and other staff need to be goal oriented and structured so that they can achieve their intended aim.

It is evident from both case studies, which the teachers in the schools discussed are in a process of transition but they need to be brought to an understanding of the four levels of functioning for the necessary paradigm shift to take place. Ideally they should function at the highest level with improved ability.

It is interesting to note that even though both schools appear to be inviting it is for different reasons. This could be attributed to the fact that different personalities have different needs. With this in mind it should be noted that messages which may be inviting to one person, are not necessarily perceived that way by another.

Conclusion

It is clear from these two case studies that the two schools are 'inviting' in concept. Many policies, programs and procedures can attain to that. Finally the following questions arise:

◆ Should not all schools in South Africa at least take note of the way schools such as the two mentioned are focused on 'moving forward'? Some of the aspects considered in this chapter will be difficult to attain by all schools, but most of the intentional values on which both schools operate are sound educational principles upon which all teaching and education have been based for centuries. If schools at least attempt to emulate some of these values, policies, programs and procedures they could be well on their way to achieving a more inviting culture.

◆ To be 'unintentionally' inviting as an educator, is not that hard given the right circumstances. When schools are managed and organized, classrooms well-equipped, teachers skilled and parents and communities involved, learners become active participants in their own development and learning. But it is not enough to be inviting 'by accident', by 'intuitively' doing what feels right, good or 'fuzzy warm'. Educators need to know what they are doing and for which reasons they are doing this consistently.

In schools such as these described the teachers may be regarded as inviting because they have a dedicated work ethic and they attribute value to their fellow man. It is however clear that being inviting at the 'surface-level' is not desirable. Both schools and their staff created situations that may be inviting to a greater or lesser extent unintentionally. For all schools in South Africa, not only independent school, a true recipe for success would be to add to their vision and mission statements a comprehensive understanding and intentional, consistent application of the theory and practice of invitational education.

Chapter 13

Creating Schools
That Invite Wellness:
A Study of Educator Perceptions
in Previously Disadvantaged Schools in South Africa

Linda C. Theron and Martyn P. van der Merve

South Africa has a history of education that has been deemed disinviting in certain respects. Historically many non-white learners were not invited to learn optimally. The results of these practices are nefarious in many senses, but especially so in terms of the wellness of learners. Currently education equity is being redressed in South Africa, but the question remains whether teachers of non-white learners understand the essence of inviting learners to experience and lead lives of wellness.

The focus of this chapter is to outline the perception which a limited number of teachers in the Vaal Triangle (Gauteng, South Africa) have of inviting wellness, and to elucidate the role of invitational education in the promotion of wellness of South African Schools.

Wellness Defined

Wellness is health broadly defined as more than the absence of disease. Rather, "... *it is a state of complete physical, mental, and social well-being*" (World Health Organization, 1997, p. 5). Thus, wellness needs to be conceived holistically: it encompasses the physical, social, mental, intellectual and spiritual dimensions of health. It is a dynamic state which is never finally attained, but which is pursued continuously over time. Similarly, the practice of wellness promotion at schools can only succeed when strategies targeting such health are comprehensive and holistic. Wellness must be intentionally invited.

The wellness promoting school recognizes this and promotes holistic health to the benefit of its learners, as well as the broader society in the long term. Attention is paid to the physical and psychosocial environment of the school as well as to the physical and psychosocial needs of the learners. This is achieved by means of flexible, multifaceted, supportive policies and practices. Wellness promoting schools emphasize a school ethos—community—curriculum link. Such partnerships invite effective, efficient and sustainable endeavors (National Framework, 2000).

Research has shown that teachers are key agents in wellness promotion, and that where teachers are intrinsically involved in and supportive of health promotion programs, the success of such programs is greater (National Framework, 2000). If wellness promotion is to succeed, educators need to understand the concept of wellness, as well as their role in the promotion thereof, and strategies which they might employ to anchor wellness. The need for a strategy to inculcate wellness is critical, hence the link to invitational education.

Invitational education is a perceptually based, self-concept approach that exhorts educators to invite learners to self-actualize (Purkey & Novak, 1996). The theory is grounded in the art of human relationships that democratically acknowledge the intrinsic value, ability and responsibility of every human being. By immersing learners in an invitational culture, wellness may be nurtured. An invitational culture and consequent wellness is intrinsic to school excellence. This is of extreme importance in the South African context with its backlogs in the educational sphere.

For this reason, invitational education is viewed by the authors as a viable vehicle for facilitating well being in schools. If educational leadership is to be truly successful, leadership will acknowledge that there are specific invitational ideals required as founding principles. There are core invitational principles which underscore the notion that education is fundamentally an imaginative act of hope aimed at inviting all stakeholders to continuously savour, understand, and better their personal and creative experiences. Of pertinence to South Africa is the emphasis in invitational education on the acknowledging that every individual is valued, able and responsible, and that education is a democratic process. The latter is of vital importance to well being in schools, given South Africa's historic educational approach of 'doing to,' rather than 'doing with.'

The Outline of the Study

A true understanding of health must be extended beyond the merely physical to the domain of holistic wellness. Invitational education aims at inculcating holistic wellness. The latter is crucial in South Africa where a myriad of learners struggle to master rudimentary education and self-actualize. In order for South Africa to achieve sustainable economic development, schools need to deliver healthy individuals who can contribute meaningfully to the development of a productive society, and experience wellness as individuals and a collective society. This will require an emphasis on inviting wellness at school level. Thus, the aim of this exploratory research was to document educator perceptions of wellness in order that strategic invitational intervention might be planned to ultimately achieve whole school excellence that would contribute to a sustainable society and individual wellness.

The broader aim can be operationalized as seeking understanding of:

◆ educators' conceptions of well-being and factors which jeopardize well-being;

◆ educators' insight into their role in the promotion of wellness;

◆ educators' opinion concerning community involvement in the promotion of wellness, i.e. their understanding of the necessity of an integral or whole school approach encompassing learner, educator and parent; and

◆ possible contributions of invitational education regarding the promotion of wellness.

Methodology

The Sample

A class of 50 honors education students was selected to participate in this investigation. The students were informed as to the aim of the exercise and consented to become involved. During their course work these students were provided with training in research methodology and then participated as field workers. The students, 44 of whom are involved in previously disadvantaged schools in the Vaal Triangle (Gauteng, South Africa), targeted the teaching staff of their schools, providing a convenience sample for the data-collection process. Typically such schools house black learners who face perennial economic and social obstacles.

Procedures

A questionnaire (in English) consisting of 7 open-ended questions concerning definitions of wellness, and school and community roles in promoting learner wellness was drawn up, following a literature study and discussion with the honors class concerning typical issues relating to wellness in their schools. The questionnaires were distributed to at least 1 school management member, 2 senior staff members (at least 5 years teaching experience) and 2 junior staff members (less than 5 years experience) which facilitated a range of responses (N = 250).

The questionnaires were distributed and completed during August and September 2001. The students reported poor co-operation from the respondents who were disinclined to commit their opinions to paper. The latter might reflect educator apathy, or alternatively educator distrust of the system, which suggests that educators need to experience Inviting leadership and management even before they will be able to disseminate Inviting messages to their learners.

Content analysis was conducted on the questionnaires. The responses were qualitatively analyzed in terms of common themes arising, and in terms of divergent views of wellness. Primarily, the researchers sought to understand how wellness is perceived and approached by local school communities, so that meaningful invitational intervention strategies might result. The common themes and differences were then contrasted to the five essential principles of the theory of invitational education.

What follows are summative tables of the core themes arising from the educator responses. Each table will be discussed in terms of teacher perceptions and the links that can be made to invitational education.

Table 1

Summary of the perceptions which educators have of the benefits of wellness promotion at school level.

The Inculcation of Wellness
◆ promotes physical health awareness
◆ promotes social upliftment
◆ promotes effective learning
◆ promotes environmental awareness
◆ promotes total development of the learner
◆ promotes sound interpersonal relations
◆ promotes a healthier community
◆ promotes community-school interaction
◆ promotes cultural/political tolerance

The above responses link strongly to the essential theory of invitational education. According to the core assumptions, when educators interact with their learners in such a way that their value, ability and responsibility are acknowledged, wellness is also fostered. The above responses allude to an unintentional understanding of the essence of invitational education. The benefit of wellness promotion is, in other words, inviting learners to become the very best learners that they can possibly be. Such self-actualization must be viewed holistically on a continuum from physical self-actualization to community self-actualization.

Table 2

Summary of the perceptions which educators have concerning the reasons that learner wellness suffers.

Factors That May Affect Wellness
◆ poor physical health
◆ malnutrition
◆ poverty
◆ ignorance
◆ poor parental involvement
◆ negative social factors
◆ emotional disturbances
◆ absence from school
◆ family problems
◆ inadequate education facilities / inadequately trained teachers
◆ inadequate extrinsic / intrinsic discipline
◆ political discrimination

When the above responses are viewed from an invitational perspective, it becomes clear that educators have become rooted in an external paradigm: inadequate wellness is perceived to result from extrinsic sources, such as poverty, poor education and inadequate facilities. The latter are valid in the third world context in which they educate. However, educators fail to understand that the process of educating is equivalent to the product and that wellness is sabotaged by inadequately emphasizing learner ability, responsibility and value. The researchers are not naively suggesting that the reality of educating in Africa be ignored, but rather that these realities be seen against the background of invitational education that provides hope despite hardship. By inviting learners to actualize their potential, wellness is championed and risk seen in a context of possibility.

Table 3

Summary of the perceptions which educators have concerning what schools are currently doing to promote wellness.

Factors that Promote Wellness
◆ Life education, life skills and motivational programs
◆ Personal hygiene, health and nutritional programs (e.g., drug awareness programs, feeding schemes; HIV education)
◆ Counseling, caring and remedial education
◆ Religious Education & social support (moral standards, biblical studies)
◆ Personal attention to learners (guidance classes)
◆ Discouraging discrimination (promoting rights, integrating different cultures)
◆ Funding (bursaries, housing donations)
◆ Pride of place (educator donations, spirit of ownership encouraged)
◆ Mentoring (adopt-a-learner campaign)
◆ Teacher professionalism (professional development: latest techniques & methodologies, seminars, conferences, study encouraged)
◆ Environmental awareness (cleaning programs; creating healthy learning environments)
◆ Twinning (collaboration between stronger and less effective schools)
◆ Collaborative management and democratic school practices (SMT, stakeholder, community involvement, parents in school management)
◆ Collaboration with the community (guardian systems, partnerships with business, pupil visitation to institutions, involvement of professionals, educators visiting homes)

The above responses suggest that educators have unintentionally grasped the importance of the five (5) P's. What is currently being done to inculcate and augment wellness, can be summarized by referring to people, places policies, programs and processes.

Table 4

Summary of the perceptions which educators have concerning community involvement in order to achieve wellness.

Community Factors that Contribute to Wellness
◆ Be responsible for education: develop learners (programs & activities, educating values, motivational talks)
◆ Support learners and teachers (professionals in community should be involved, shared expertise and knowledge safe surroundings, society of equal opportunity, interventionist role)
◆ Acknowledge social responsibility (feeding schemes; establish community centers; building schools; funding)
◆ Initiate health awareness
◆ Acknowledge learner rights
◆ Arrange workshops and clinics (encourage communication of health issues; supporting HIV-positive persons; combating drugs, crime and vandalism)
◆ Encourage democratic practices (greater involvement of learners in the community)
◆ Encourage collaboration (working committees, partnerships with schools) Clean the environment (desist from dumping garbage outside school; volunteer to clean schools)
◆ Function as role models (social and cultural ideology must support education)

The above responses suggest that educators do acknowledge the need for community collaboration, but the researchers note that in some instances, educators appear almost too reliant on community involvement, thereby sabotaging the true nature of collaboration. Significantly, the community is perceived as a source of support, but educators do not mention the reciprocity of such support. Especially in Africa, where many parents are illiterate and unskilled, schools should also be inviting towards community stakeholders in order to build capacity and sustain development. Wellness cannot be nurtured in an environment that is not systemic.

The Strategic Role of Invitational Education

What is heartening about the above responses is a general positive attitude towards inviting wellness. Significantly, the teachers polled in this study have no prior exposure to the theory of invitational education, yet their responses allude to an unintentional understanding of the core principles of invitational education. The focus must be to make this understanding both intentional and comprehensively inclusive of all five principles.

When the teachers' responses are analyzed in terms of the core principles of invitational education, the following becomes apparent:

The First Core Principle

People are valued, regarded as able and responsible and should be treated accordingly.

◆ The teachers' (respondents) responses in this probe clearly point to an intuitive understanding of the importance of this principle. Teachers' support the notion of wellness as invitational and underscores the idea that stakeholders are so valuable, able and responsible, that their wellness matters. Health and physical well-being of learners, personal attention to learners, mentoring of learners, supporting learners, acknowledging their rights and acting as role models are themes that support this finding. Teachers are also aware of the negative aspects that influence learners' development like poverty, malnutrition, inadequate motivation and political discrimination, but fail to have faith in the personal abilities and responsibility of the learners. Their sense that these risk factors lead to wellness suffering, suggests that they understand that risk factors sabotage stakeholders' ability to respond to invitational messages. The fact that teachers view the community as part and parcel of education, suggests that responsibility for education must be shared. The latter is vital in a South African context, where the notion of UBUNTU is fundamental to the African way of life. UBUNTU is a spirit of sharing and acknowledging that one is only a person within the collective domain of other persons. In other words, the responsibility for education is a collective one.

◆ It does seem, however, that the respondents do not place strong emphasis on the active role that the learners play in their own learning and development. This may be due to the aggressive role-played by student representative bodies and the active role taken by youth organizations in the South African context. Learners need to be allowed to take greater responsibility for their own learning—a notion which very easily fits with the emphasis on Outcome-Based teaching and the Constructivist learning paradigm. Learners should also be allowed to be co-participants in their own learning. It appears that teachers involved in this research still adhere to the more traditional teaching style, where teachers are in control of the learners' learning, and learners are passive recipients.

◆ Teachers' responses suggest that wellness is important and should be striven for. Theoretically, by acknowledging the significance of wellness, learner potential is understood and learners are seen as valuable beings who should be invited to self-actualize—wellness inherently suggests self-actualization. When learners are invited to self-actualize, their intrinsic potential is acknowledged. What is missing, however, from teachers' lists of what schools can do to encourage wellness, is an explicit reference to inviting learners and stakeholders to be the very best that they can possibly be, and indeed better than they currently are. Teachers can conceptualize using programs and feeding schemes and so on to invite learners, but they do not have the expertise to understand that exhorting learners to self-actualize and achieve wellness begins with teacher perception and teacher attitude. There is no reference to an attitude of trust or optimism, or to perceiving stakeholders as beings with relatively untapped potential. Every learner needs to be valued as an intelligent and worthwhile human being. Consequently opportunities must be created for them to decide on themes within the curriculum, outcomes to be reached that they will experience as relevant, activities for these outcomes to be met, and criteria for assessing their learning and opportunities to reflect on the process and future learning.

It is clear from the responses by the teachers that little understanding of the crucial interpersonal relationship between teacher and learner is forthcoming. As long as teachers view teaching as a 'one-directional activity' influenced and managed externally, learners will experience their time at school as disinviting, irrelevant and even confrontational.

The Second Core Principle
Education should be a collaborative, cooperative activity.

◆ As indicated above, this is an important principle according to most contemporary views of education worldwide. What is positive is teachers' sense of the need for collaboration with the community in order to achieve wellness—a process of collaboration will encourage a healthy product. By inviting community participation, learners are encouraged to be well in their total context, and not just at school.

◆ In this case, the participants in this probe have indicated that community-school interaction, poor parental involvement, inadequate facilities, twinning between schools, collaborative management, parental involvement in management, and collaboration with the community are ways to ensure the existence of this principle. These teachers seem to regard collaboration as a process that takes place between the school and the outside world. Schools, teachers and management, collaborate with stakeholders in the community. Collaboration in the form of guardian systems, learner visits to institutions, educators visiting homes and twinning of schools focus on the development of the learners. It is, however, noticeable that the collaboration and cooperative spirit in the classroom between teachers and learners is not mentioned. Without teacher-learner collaboration, education remains a 'doing-to' process, rather than a 'doing-with.'

Good collaboration with the community does exist according to the respondents. Professionals and experts getting involved, health education, partnerships with schools, environmental responsibility and learner involvement in community issues are some of the themes mentioned. One should, however, guard against an abdication of responsibility by educators in this respect. Education is a relationship between the teacher and learners in the first and final instance. Communities can support and collaborate, but the teachers and the school needs to establish a culture of collaboration and cooperation in the school.

Collaboration between teachers in the school, cooperative learning opportunities amongst learners in the same class, between different classes, and even different grades may be established. Collaboration and cooperation aimed at developing each and every learner seems to be lacking in the responses of the participants.

The Third Core Principle
The process of education is the product in the making.

◆ In the invitational sense this principle means everything matters. Every word, every action is part of the end result in education. Themes that tend to support an understanding of this principle are: promotion of social upliftment, total development of the learners, a healthier community, life education and life skills programs, social support, integration of different cultures and religions, healthy living environments and collaboration with communities and other institutions. It does appear, however, that the participants in this research do not show a clear understanding of the systemic nature of an inviting approach to education. Many of the themes identified appear detached and compartmentalized. The latter links to an inadequate understanding of the process being equal to the product in the making. How teachers interact with learners can invite wellness, or sabotage the very essence thereof. No matter how intentionally driven wellness-programs are, without a fundamental belief in the holistic process of inviting learners, the process will not result in a product that testifies to wellness. If education aims at developing the people involved, then all activities need to be planned and coordinated to achieve this aim. This applies to all those involved, not only to the learners. Teachers, parents and the general community should be involved and benefit from this process.

The Fourth Core Principle
People possess untapped potential in all areas of human endeavor.

◆ This belief does not develop clearly from the identified themes in this study. Participants in this research regard external factors more dominant than a belief in human potential. Poor physical health, malnutrition, ignorance, family problems, inadequate facilities, etc. are mentioned (refer to table 2) as factors which cause wellness to suffer. An optimistic view of the human spirit and potential seems to be lacking. Mention is made though, of supporting learners in their development, acknowledging learners' rights and encouraging democratic practices by involving learners in the communities, which alludes to the latent potential of the learners. The latter implies that learners will benefit from exposure to programs which encourage the development of potential—in other words, learner potential is indirectly acknowledged.

217

◆ More is required than just programs though. Teachers in these schools need to affirm the belief that the learners 'CAN'. Teacher attitude is of vital importance in this regard—verbal and non-verbal messages regarding teachers' unconditional belief in learner worth are essential if learners are to believe in their untapped potential. Specific opportunities for learners to develop different areas of potential will also need to be planned. With the current drive towards OBE and the revised Curriculum 2005 teachers are being trained to facilitate learning rather than 'providing' learning through their own teaching. Underlying this philosophy is the belief that learners learn more effectively in learning-oriented classrooms where learners are the active participants in their own learning as well as the 'managers' of their own learning process. In real terms this may imply that learners be given opportunities to decide what they want to learn about a certain topic, how they want to learn about it, how and when they want to be assessed about their learning. This assumes a tremendous mind-shift for teachers. It assumes that the educator becomes part of the process rather than the driver of the process, and democratically participates and experiences the learning process taking place in the classroom. In this way more options for learning and the acknowledgement of different learning styles and preferences may be accommodated, which in turn infers belief in learner potential to actively participate.

◆ The themes identified from this study indicate a lack of understanding of this principle. If teachers do not understand that people possess untapped potential, there is a danger that their ability to act invitingly will be sabotaged, given the interdependence of the five core principles.

The Fifth Core Principle
The potential can best be realized by places, policies, programs and processes designed to invite development; and by people who

are intentionally inviting with themselves and others personally and professionally.

◆ The participants in this study appeared to have a partial understanding of this principle. They do acknowledge the role of places in this regard. Places are acknowledged when they refer to cleaning the environment—the latter is especially pertinent to the township schools where this research was conducted: schools are generally unkempt and ramshackle with a minimum of equipment and characterized by litter. Furthermore, establishing community centres, safe surroundings, adequate facilities, pride of place (where even educators give donations and a spirit of ownership is encouraged) are some of the themes that indicate an awareness of the important role of the physical surroundings to creating wellness.

◆ A number of themes which relate to programs, policies and processes are also mentioned. Life education, life skills and motivational programs; personal hygiene, health and nutritional programs; counseling, caring and remedial education programs and policies; religious education; personal attention to learners; discouraging discrimination; funding and twinning of schools are themes which indicate an awareness of these aspects of the principle. It is, however, noticeable that the respondents do not manage to integrate the many policies mentioned, which may allude to an inability to understand the holistic nature of wellness promotion and invitational education. They also do not indicate that these programs, policies and processes are planned and focused on the development of wellness that may allude to unintentional invitational behavior, rather than intentional acts.

This principle also asks for people who are intentionally inviting towards themselves and others, personally and professionally to become reality. In the responses by the participants the following themes are noted:

◆ parents and the family: a need for parental involvement, a decrease in family problems (poverty, etc.) is needed, parents are involved in school management, functioning as role models socially and culturally;

◆ community: professionals share expertise and give motivational talks;

◆ teachers: professional development of teachers through study, seminars and conferences.

It is clear from these responses that an emphasis on people is encouraged. It appears, however, as if these interventions are motivated externally—a 'doing-to' approach—rather than a personal motivation from those involved. It also seems as if few invitations are sent to others to develop themselves personally and professionally.

Educators who wish to promote wellness need to create opportunities for their learners to develop holistically, which is personally and professionally. In addition they have to care for themselves, to motivate themselves on a personal and professional level. Their involvement in the community should be one of allowing parents and community members to participate fully in this process. It is clear from the responses that the participants do not actually understand the role that people play in the holistic process of wellness promotion and invitational living and that their responses indicate an intuitive and unintentional understanding of this concept.

Conclusion

It was found that the teachers polled are unintentionally inviting in the manner in which they think about wellness. Teachers conceive peripherally that learners are valuable, able, and responsible—what they do not quite manage to portray in their responses is that learners should also be *treated* as if they are valuable, able, and responsible. The teacher's beliefs do not appear to translate into actions.

Teachers in this study also grasped the concept that collaboration is essential if learners are to be invited towards wellness. Community co-operation is strongly emphasized. What is perhaps not strongly emphasized is the reciprocal nature of such collaboration. Teachers may not abdicate the responsibility for educating to the community, nor may the community wash its hands of the process. Rather, a symbiotic 'doing with' approach is needed. The process of educating for wellness is confined to a plethora of programs. Teachers fail to indicate that such programs are additive to the invitations which they need to send continuously, and that the programs themselves may not equal the process. Invitational education is a theory of practice—the process is ongoing and holistic. Clearly, the latter is not adequately understood.

Learner potential is alluded to, but the researchers are not convinced that the teachers polled truly understand the essence of this essential principle. Learners need to be overtly and indirectly invited on a continual basis. The five P's are unintentionally acknowledged: places, programs, policies and procedures more so than people. Teachers appear to understand the 5 P's as a fragmented concept, rather than as a gestalt.

These findings suggest that teachers have intuitively grasped aspects of invitational education, but lack a comprehensive, detailed understanding. This deficit will make it impossible for them to use invitational education as a strategy to create schools which invite wellness. In order to invite learners and stakeholders to be educated optimally, teachers require formal training in invitational education in order to become intentionally inviting.

Recommendations for creating invitational schools in previously disadvantaged areas of South Africa can be made from the invitational education paradigm, which include:

◆ Focusing on learner health and wellness during formal teacher training;

◆ Providing in-service teacher training concerning invitational teacher perceptions, invitational teacher stance, and invitational practice;

◆ Assisting whole school development towards health promotion by using the invitational education Helix model.

◆ Establishment of mentor teachers who adhere to invitational education principles to foster wellness of other educators and learners.

Specifically, to create Inviting schools in previously disadvantaged communities, teachers need to:

◆ Accept the value of invitational interaction with learners.

◆ Translate invitational belief into invitational action.

◆ Acknowledge symbiotic reciprocity with educational stakeholders, including the community.

◆ Intentionally invite themselves and other stakeholders to achieve wellness.

◆ Conceptualize invitational educational activity holistically.

The peripheral responses of the respondents provide convincing support of a lack of comprehensive understanding of wellness, and perhaps also, a lack of commitment towards wellness. This highlights the need for emphasis at school level on holistic health promotion, as well as confirmation of the pivotal role which invitational education has to play in achieving school excellence and ultimately empowering previously disadvantaged and minority communities. If South Africa is to flourish, schools may not ignore their crucial role in inviting wellness.

References

Australian Health Promoting Schools Association. (2000) *A National framework for health promoting schools* (2000-2003). Brisbane: Policy Document

Purkey, W.W. & Novak, J.M. (1996). *Inviting school success: A self-concept approach to teaching, learning and democratic practice* (Third Edition). Toronto: Wadsworth

World Health Organization. (1997). *Promoting health through schools.* Geneva: World Health Organization.

Chapter 14

Reaffirmation of Re-Accreditation through Invitational Education

Deborah Lonon

How does a "Superior-rated" learning institution become even better? That was the question facing Asheville-Buncombe Technical Community College in Asheville, North Carolina, as the lengthy process to reaffirm re-accreditation began. One of the first to utilize the Southern Association of Colleges and Schools' newly-revised Principles of Accreditation, A-B Tech soon learned that a key accreditation component, the "Quality Enhancement Plan" was now a requirement. This "QEP" and the process for deriving it had several major caveats: it must focus specifically on an important student learning issue; that issue must be determined through a recursive, comprehensive process unique to each institution's culture; it must be creative, far-reaching and college-transforming!

Each of these daunting requirements was met through A-B Tech's use of invitational education. Our QEP topic, "Educational and Career Advisement," was selected through a broad-based, inclusive, College-wide effort centered on the tenets of invitational education; this QEP was fully accepted and approved by SACS with no recommendations. Not only that, the SACS on-site visiting team noted during their exit interview that A-B Tech was well on its way to becoming a "beacon" institution for modeling invitational education. Here's how it happened.

Background

A-B Tech Programs and Services

With three campuses (serving one in three residents of Buncombe and Madison counties), A-B Tech is a comprehensive community college located in beautiful western North Carolina that began as the Asheville Industrial Education Center in 1959. Three initial programs were offered: practical nursing, electronics engineering, and machining. Today, those three programs continue to be offered along with numerous other career and college transfer programs, currently totaling forty-nine (49).

The College offers the Associate in Arts, the Associate in Science, and the Associate in Applied Science degrees, diplomas and certificates. In August of 2003, the Associate in Fine Arts was offered for the first time. More than 8,000 students are enrolled in the curriculum programs and nearly 19,000 in continuing education classes. Since 1995-96, overall enrollment is up more than 47 percent, with continuing education experiencing a 58 percent increase and curriculum nearly 26 percent. Between 1997 and 2002, A-B Tech's annual FTE jumped nearly 41 percent in continuing education and more than 36 percent in curriculum.

Both curriculum and continuing education programs are supported through the activities of the GED Testing program, Developmental Studies, and the Learning Resources Center. A-B Tech provides a number of academic support services such as: academic advising, academic support labs, career counseling (through the Career Center and through the one-credit hour student success course, ACA-115), college transfer advising, computer lab services, placement testing, research assistance at the Learning Resource Center, services to students with disabilities, and supplemental instruction and tutoring. In addition, A-B Tech provides ceremonies and other means to recognize academic achievement, on-site and televised academic orientation; co-curricular activities to any academic program which chooses to establish a student organization, emergency personal counseling, financial aid assistance, child care assistance, transfer advisement and articulation, and veterans' counseling.

A-B Tech's dedication to students and their success over the past 40+ years of its history may be seen in our succinct mission statement: *A-B Tech, the community's college, is dedicated to student success. As a comprehensive community college, A-B Tech is committed to providing accessible, quality educational opportunities for lifelong learning to meet the diverse and changing needs of our community.*

A-B Tech's "Superior" Rating

The North Carolina General Assembly has, for the third consecutive year, designated A-B Tech as a "Superior College" based on such criteria as the employment rate of graduates (99.76%*), the percentage of students who indicate they achieved their educational goal (100%*), the passing rate of students in developmental courses (92%*), and the performance of college transfer students after one year at a public university. Regarding this last indicator, it is important to note that 96.7%* of A- B Tech transfer students achieved a grade point average of 2.0 or above after two semesters at a UNC institution, the highest rating for this indicator from a community college in North Carolina.

Since the quality enhancement planning process began, A-B Tech has been one of only three colleges in the fifty-eight North Carolina Community College System to earn the "Superior" designation for three consecutive years. While this honor clearly reflects the outstanding qualities of our institution's faculty, staff, and students, it also indicates the dilemma faced at the start of the QEP process: there was no immediate, obvious area of needed improvement. That's where invitational education came into the picture.

* These percentages are from 2003.

QEP Process

Immediately following receipt of the New Principles of Accreditation, a SACS Leadership Team was formed at A-B Tech, consisting of the President, Vice President for Instruction, Vice President for Student Services, SACS Liaison, Institutional Effectiveness Council Chair and Quality Enhancement Plan Team Leader. Next, the President appointed the Quality Enhancement Team, a 16-member committee representing every college work group, department or division and the Student Government Association. Charged with guiding the planning process for developing the QEP, each team member agreed to be the primary contact person for his/her area, and to represent that group's perspective, along with serving as champion for the QEP.

The first step of A-B Tech's QEP process was a College-wide review of our current, five-year strategic plan, followed by initial recommendations for a topic. Common themes included student success, "operationalizing" our mission statement, retention, and student transition between curriculum and continuing education. These recommendations were discussed and incorporated into the topic, "In a climate of constant change, how can we create an adaptable learning environment that promotes student success?" This topic was further refined to "Developing Strategies for Student Success" and forwarded to the Quality Enhancement Team.

Much time and energy were devoted to discovering a way to approach it (beginning with an attempt to first define "student success" and then determine a way to measure it!) The QE Team was temporarily stalled and somewhat stymied, but not discouraged. Several meetings later, one of the Team members (Dr. Deborah Harmon, an active member of the International Alliance for Invitational Education and Director of Counseling at A-B Tech) suggested the idea of using invitational education as a way to approach the development of student success strategies. This one, simple idea led to the following:

◆ an in-depth study of invitational education and its practices

◆ a College-wide effort to become more "invitational"

◆ a new, expanded view of the College and its campuses as a single learning environment (and of every employee as an "advisor")

◆ a QEP centered on invitational education tenets

◆ a recommendation-free SACS exit report

◆ the honor of being designated an "Inviting School!"

Invitational Education

Readers of this text are probably already familiar with the basic tenets of invitational education. As a reminder, according to Novak and Purkey (2001), invitational education is a theory of practice with the goal of creating a total school environment that intentionally and cordially summons success for everyone associated with that school. Upon closer examination, the goals of the QEP and invitational education are similarly aligned: their intent is to provide a positive plan, unique to the institution, which promotes possibilities for successful student learning.

Because A-B Tech's own mission and institutional effectiveness processes are dedicated to and measured by student success, the Quality Enhancement Team viewed invitational education as a viable model for addressing the College's approach to helping students achieve their educational goals. Four basic premises apply to invitational education:

1. Education is a cooperative, collaborative activity where process is as important as the product.

2. People are able, valuable, and responsible and should be treated accordingly.

3. People possess untapped potential in all areas of human endeavor.

4. Human potential can best be realized by places, policies, programs and processes specifically designed to invite development, and by people who are intentionally inviting with themselves and others, personally, and professionally.

The International Alliance for Invitational Education (IAIE), founded in 1982 by Dr. William W. Purkey and Dr. Betty L. Siegel, includes 1000 members (representing twelve countries) who seek to apply the concepts of invitational education to their personal and professional lives. The Alliance's mission is to enhance life-long learning, promote positive changes in organizations, cultivate the personal and professional growth and satisfaction of educators and allied professionals, and enrich the lives of human beings personally and professionally. A-B Tech became an institutional member of the IAIE in 2003.

Proponents of invitational education sincerely and strongly believe that there is a direct correlation between the "Inviting" college and student success. While the implementation of invitational education may be a complex process, it involves one simple idea: intentionality. The Quality Enhancement Team at A-B Tech recommended utilizing invitational education in the quality enhancement planning process due to its:

◆ emphasis on the student's role in the learning process

◆ embrace of varying learning styles and other diversity issues

◆ strong match with A-B Tech's mission statement (especially student success and lifelong learning)

◆ role as a potential retention-increaser

◆ support by respected scholars, literature and a national alliance of members.

Because invitational education was chosen as the means through which to review and develop additional student success strategies, A-B Tech's quality enhancement planning process called for a view of the entire campus as a "learning environment." What does that mean? It means that every person employed at A-B Tech plays a part in student success, and everything that happens at A-B Tech affects the learning environment. The Quality Enhancement Team did not want to limit a QEP to the classroom for several reasons. First, they already knew that A-B Tech's faculty is exceptionally talented and creative. A-B Tech's performance measures clearly show that students who leave our classrooms and programs are thoroughly prepared for employment or further study. Second, the QEP instructions emphasized a very broad-based approach. Selecting a QEP related only to the classroom would leave out a large number of other employees, all of whom experience interactions with students every single day. This inclusive approach to the QEP also supports invitational education's belief that "...those who are affected by decisions should have a say in those decisions" (Novak & Purkey, 2001). For the QEP to meet its stated goal of college-wide consensus, every employee needed to be involved in the selection of the QEP topic.

In its discussion of "learning and success," the Quality Enhancement Team reasoned that no student could ultimately achieve success without first gaining accurate and up-to-date advisement information about what programs are offered and how to register for those programs. Therefore, A-B Tech's "learning environment" extended all the way out to the parking lot; if a student couldn't find a place to park, if the buildings and room numbers were not properly labeled and easy to locate, then simply finding the correct building upon arrival might ultimately affect a student's chance for attaining success at our College. What these Team members had figured out correlates directly with the established 5 "P's" of invitational education—the People, Places, Policies, Programs and Processes. Looking at A-B Tech through the lens of invitational education allowed the Quality Enhancement Team to propose the following definition of student/learning success: "a change in the knowledge, skills and/or behavior that facilitates the attainment of education and career goals."

Invitational Awareness at A-B Tech

According to Purkey and Novak (1993), "creating an inviting education institution requires a sound understanding of key ideas and a willingness to put them into practice in imaginative and collaborative ways." Their "invitational helix" was designed to facilitate that process. According to the helix, a commitment to invitational education moves from awareness, to understanding, to application, to adoption and that is what has happened at A-B Tech over the past two years. While the process is still evolving, and there are some employees who continue to think that being "invitational" means being "nice" and "giving all students A's," many more are aware of the true goals, understand them, and seek to actively apply them to both their professional and personal lives. This helix began at A-B Tech with the selection of "Developing Strategies for Student Success through Invitational Education" as the original QEP theme.

To introduce this theme to the College, the QET began planning the first of three Quality Enhancement Retreats. Utilizing an afternoon already set aside for professional development activities, the first retreat was scheduled for September 19, 2002 and was designed with four goals in mind:

1. Develop a positive attitude about invitational education

2. Understand the correlation between the "inviting" college and student success

3. Learn about the "5 P's" of invitational education (People, Places, Programs, Policies, and Processes)

4. Identify, using appreciative inquiry, specific ways that A-B Tech is inviting

Much time and effort was spent making the afternoon "invitational" even before attendees heard the word for the first time. The Quality Enhancement Team and the SACS Liaison worked to devise clear goals and expectations, and these were effectively communicated to the College-wide community. Several colorful and enticing announcements about the upcoming retreat were developed and sent out by the SACS Liaison to create interest. Official "greeters" waved employees into the parking lot and walked with them to the front door. Music was playing and balloons were flying. A catered lunch was provided, and each person was asked to bring a dessert to share, an idea that caught on and was appreciated by everyone who enjoyed the many delicious and varied offerings. Further, by utilizing an afternoon already scheduled for professional development activities, employees felt that their time was valued.

The "5-P" Relay, Part I

On that beautiful, clear September afternoon, over 400 College employees as well as representatives of the Student Government Association gathered to hear more about the QEP and the theme, "Developing Strategies for Student Success." For many, it was the first opportunity to hear about invitational education. Others remembered William Purkey's stirring invitational education presentation from a professional development activity a few years earlier.

After socializing, eating and receiving a warm greeting from the SACS liaison and the QEP Team Leader, this large assemblage received directions on participating in the "5-P" Relay. This term was unfamiliar to all but the Quality Enhancement Team and caused a bit of uncertainty. In fact, one faculty member asked if that was "a race to the restroom!" Participants soon learned that "5-P" Relay is an invitational education strategy designed to identify invitational strengths and challenges, and to set "invitational" goals, face obstacles, and develop plans for successful implementation. The Relay was conducted in two parts and served as an integral component of both the first and second Quality Enhancement Retreats. Appreciative inquiry (focusing on what's already going well and finding ways to duplicate those efforts) was chosen as the approach for this first retreat, since it allowed the College community to intentionally focus in on what was already "inviting" about A-B Tech rather than on "problem-solving."

Employees were divided into eight groups of fifty. Each of the eight groups was located in a room with five tables, one table for each "P." The following text was posted at each table:

People

In planning efforts that improve the quality of life for the PEOPLE of our college, we can ask ourselves how we see ourselves and our students, how we envision our relations with each other and how we can extend and nurture those caring relationships in ways that summon forth human potential.

Listed below are "Inviting" characteristics of A-B Tech personnel (trusting, inclusive, diverse, respectful, optimistic, accessible, courteous, intentional, caring). Name a time when you have observed someone displaying this kind of behavior. When have you seen someone helping a student succeed? What happened?

Places

In considering improvements regarding PLACES, we can examine our facilities and grounds and find ways to enhance the total physical environment of the college. Is this a place where people want to be and want to learn? In most schools, places are the easiest factors to change. They offer opportunities for immediate improvement.

Listed below are "Inviting" characteristics of places (functional, attractive, clean, efficient, aesthetic, personal, warm). How do visitors to our campus know that A-B Tech is a caring and cared-for environment?

Programs

In planning or revising PROGRAMS, we can be more innovative in finding ways to create more meaningful connections with our students, the curriculum and the world around us.

Listed below are examples of broadly defined programs at A-B Tech. Do they meet the needs of our students and our community? How do we know they are meeting those needs? How many of these programs are you aware of? How are their ideals/goals communicated to staff and students? How do you find out more about them?

Policies

Given the importance of the language we use to describe our operations and expectations, POLICIES become critical "semantic webs" that shape the spirit of the school. When policies are perceived as fair, inclusive, democratic, and respectful, they will have a positive effect on people's attitudes.

Listed below are a few examples of written and unwritten procedures, codes or rules used to regulate the ongoing functions of individuals and organizations at A-B Tech. Name some examples of policies that are written and communicated in an "inviting" manner (i.e., fair, inclusive, democratic, respectful.). Do you know where to find policies at A-B Tech? Are they easily and clearly understood once found?

Processes

The very PROCESSES we employ to transform schools need to be democratically inviting in and of themselves. How we go about creating a more exciting, satisfying, and enriching college becomes as important as defining the inviting college we want to become.

Listed below are examples of processes at A-B Tech: committee work, academic orientation, advising, registration, duplicating, promotional materials, mailing, placement testing, purchasing supplies, new faculty orientation, interdisciplinary teaming, networking, employee evaluation, mentoring. How many of these reflect a cooperative spirit, democratic activities, and ethical guidelines?

Facilitated by Quality Enhancement Team members, each table participated in an icebreaking activity and the selection of a note taker. Then, using the appreciative inquiry approach described above, each table examined and discussed their particular "P" (People, Places, etc.) for up to fifteen minutes. After time was called, attendees from table one moved to table two, etc. The Relay ended after one and a half hours. The QET distributed detailed results (along with requests for feedback and comments) to the College community through campus e-mail, postings and publication in A-B Tech's newsletter, *TechTalk*.

Utilizing the appreciative inquiry approach allowed for a focus on the positive, and kept the Relay participants from falling into a "griping" session (that never happens at your institution, does it?) Facilitators continually brought participants back to the positive, but did allow for discussion of "challenges" that inevitably arose. These "challenges" were all related to student success, directly or indirectly. Here are the top three:

1. Reduce waiting time in the advising/registration process.

2. Improve communication across all campuses (includes improving signage on buildings and classrooms, and the need for a "Central Information System" to be accessed by the entire college).

3. Improve parking.

Immediately following the Quality Enhancement Retreat I, the QET leader and members participated in many invitational education awareness activities across the College. They attended department/division meetings, employee meetings and student organization meetings to provide information and handouts and to answer questions about invitational education, its basic premises and its intentionality. Further information and updates on invitational education and its role in the quality enhancement planning process were provided through bulletin board displays, e-mail updates, Board of Trustee and Foundation presentations, general employee meeting updates, faculty meeting updates, *TechTalk* newsletter articles and a column on inviting activities related to the QEP called the "Q-Tips" column. Additionally, the College offered the program, "Resolving Conflict through Invitational Education" for both the classroom and the work place. A special session was held for office professionals, who play a key role in student interaction on our College's three campuses.

"5-P" Relay, Part II

Designed to build upon "invitational" information conveyed and gathered from the first retreat, the QE Retreat II continued the "5-P" Relay—this time focusing on "Invitability" challenges at A-B Tech and ways to meet those challenges.

The 400 participants were divided into groups of 20-30 and assigned to classrooms. Rather than moving from table to table as in the first QE Retreat "5-P" Relay, the group collectively discussed People, Places, Programs, Policies and Processes. Each QET facilitator used an individualized approach to discuss the topics and move towards a group consensus; however, the outcomes were standardized. After reading and discussing the texts reprinted below, each group was asked to perform three tasks:

1. Brainstorm and list other challenges related to that particular "P"

2. Select the Top 3 challenges for that "P"

3. Suggest some potential solutions to these "P" challenges.

Topic #1—People

In planning efforts that improve the quality of life for the PEOPLE of our college, we can ask ourselves how we see ourselves and our students, how we envision our relations with each other and how we can extend and nurture those caring relationships in ways that summon forth human potential.

At the QE Retreat I we asked: When our A-B Tech people are at their best, what's going on? Answers were overwhelmingly positive. A few examples: every student is served, students feel comfortable in seeking help for problems, faculty and staff go beyond the "Call of Duty" to assist students and each other, and the college mission statement is positive and inclusive. Here are some "Challenges" that were listed: address advising/teaching load, determine where a student needs to go before sending him/her across campus, reduce time spent in advising/registration lines, centralize location of student registration, bookstore and business office, and clearly define all positions with job descriptions/ensure duties are consistent for similar positions across campus.

Topic #2—Places

In considering improvements regarding PLACES, we can examine our facilities and grounds and find ways to enhance the total physical environment of the college. Is this a place where people want to be and want to learn? In most schools, places are the easiest factors to change. They offer opportunities for immediate improvement.

At the first QE Retreat, we asked: "Is A-B Tech a place where people want to be and want to learn?" A few examples: landscaping and grounds are well maintained and attractive, classroom instructional equipment is up to date, Beech Tree Deck is centrally located and provides a gathering place. Some "Challenges" listed were: provide covered, designated smoking areas to avoid trash, pollution, and second-hand smoke, provide study/gathering areas for students and employees in all buildings, clearly mark all buildings and room numbers, centralize location of student registration, bookstore and business office, and provide additional food choices during both day and evening.

Topic #3—Programs

In planning or revising PROGRAMS, we can be more innovative in finding ways to create more meaningful connections with our students, the curriculum and the world around us.

At the first QE Retreat, we asked, "How many A-B Tech programs are you already aware of?" Those listed: special needs, career counseling, Super Tuesday, GED, and CISCO. Challenges noted were: adjunct instructor orientation, training programs for staff and faculty on technology use, and awareness of curriculum and continuing education offerings.

Topic #4—Policies

Given the importance of the language we use to describe our operations and expectations, POLICIES become critical "semantic webs" that shaped the spirit of the school. When policies are perceived as fair, inclusive, democratic, and respectful, they will have a positive effect on people's attitudes.

At the first QE Retreat, we asked, "How can we make A-B Tech policies more inclusive, encouraging, and involving?" Those listed: A-B Tech has clearly defined policies on vacation, sick days, shared leave, student admissions and student code of conduct. Challenges listed: sick leave/vacation benefits to adjunct instructors, child care services on a priority basis to students and faculty, and consistent interpretation and documentation of policies across campus.

Topic #5—Processes

The very PROCESSES we employ to transform schools need to be democratically inviting in and of themselves. How we go about creating a more exciting, satisfying, and enriching college becomes as important as defining the inviting college we want to become.

At the first QE Retreat, we asked, "How many processes at A-B Tech reflect a cooperative spirit, democratic activities, and ethical guidelines?" Further, "How are decisions made here?" "Who decides how things will happen?" "How are decisions communicated to us?" "Do we feel we've been a part of the process in these decisions?" Those listed: numbers continue to rise and every student is served, CPT testing is very invitational and free, advising is distributed across campus, and promotional materials represent diverse programs. Challenges listed: reduce waiting time/long lines in advising/registration, provide e-mail addresses for adjunct faculty, clarify and reduce time spent on purchasing supplies, provide more training opportunities for faculty advisors, devise system that compensates for absence of 9-month faculty during advising periods.

While the Arts and Science Division met with full-time employees and faculty, the QET Leader conducted a special session on "Invitability" for adjunct instructors in that division. After completing the Invitational Education Employee Survey (described below), attendees gathered for a keynote address by Betty Siegel, co-founder of the International Alliance for Invitational Education. Siegel delivered an ovation-inducing speech about the influential role of invitational education in her more than twenty years as president of Kennesaw State University as well as in her personal life. According to Siegel, a college campus can and should become an environment in which employees and students are encouraged to view education as a cooperative, collaborative activity where process is as important as product. She declared that every A-B Tech employee is a "teacher" who plays a significant role in the success of A-B Tech's students. Siegel talked about the theory behind invitational education, and how it was much more than "just being nice." This distinction has been fully addressed in *Becoming an Invitational Leader: A New Approach to Professional and Personal Success* Purkey and Siegel (2003):

> Invitational education is at heart a moral activity, intentionally expressing respect and trust in ourselves and others, personally and professionally. It is both optimistic and realistic. It is not about sugar-coated palliatives regarding the power of positive thinking or about tossing gratuitous compliments or praise at every opportunity. It is about applying a particular theory of democratic practice, and doing so with fullest and best intentions to nurture a decent and caring society. (p. 19)

A-B Tech Invitational Education Curriculum Student Survey

In order to assess A-B Tech's students' perceptions of the College's "Invitability," the Quality Enhancement Team wrote and pilot-tested a 50-question survey. After receiving permission from Dr. William Purkey, this survey was based on the "Inviting School Survey," which assesses the role of the 5 "P's" in achieving school success. Questions relating to A-B Tech's People, Places, Programs, Policies and Processes were included, along with ample space for comments.

The "A-B Tech Invitational Education Curriculum Student Survey" was distributed on Wednesday, February 13, 2003 to all students enrolled in class at either 10:00 a.m. or 6:00 p.m. Of the 2,674 students enrolled during those time periods, responses were received from 1,424, for a return rate of 53% (This is approximately 27% of the 5,328 total students enrolled during Spring Semester 2003.)

Student responses were overwhelmingly positive in support of A-B Tech's staff, faculty and learning environment. I.E. Curriculum Student Survey results showed the following areas of concern (See Table 1).

Table 1
Survey Results

Curriculum Student Survey Results	Does Not Meet or Somewhat Meets
1. When I ask for information or assistance on campus, college employees are able to provide it for me."	12%
3. "When I leave messages through the college voice mail system, I receive a prompt and clear response to my message."	27%
5."My academic advisor works one on one with me to help me achieve my educational goals."	23%
6. "My academic advisor is usually available to speak with me when I need him/her."	19%
Curriculum Student Survey Results	Does Not Meet or Somewhat Meets
17. When registering for classes, I know where to go and whom to see."	13%
27. "I received a syllabus (course outline) on the first day of class."	3%
28.b "I can find what I need on the A-B Tech website."	15%

41. "I can be seen by my advisor in a reasonable amount of time."	18%
42, My advisor provides effective advising on course selection, program requirements, transfer information."	19%
44. "The registration process operates smoothly."	28%
48. "I am comfortable asking A-B Tech employees questions if I don't understand something."	10%

At the end of the survey, students were asked, "Out of the questions asked, which ONE do you consider the most important to your success as a student at A-B Tech?" and "What have we forgotten to ask that you really want us to know?" Concerns expressed by students centered around "comfort" issues: food offerings, parking, designated smoking and non-smoking areas, cleanliness/maintenance of bathrooms and buildings, and places to gather and study. Many of these items have been addressed during the QEP process, and a list of these is provided in a few pages.

A-B Tech Invitational Education
Employee Survey

Designed to assess A-B Tech's "Invitability," the Employee Invitational Education Survey asked 57 questions related to People, Places, Programs, Policies and Processes, including ample space for additional comments. At the end of the survey, participants were asked, "Out of the questions asked, which one do you consider the most important?" and "What have we forgotten to ask that you really wanted us to know." As mentioned earlier, all attendees at the second Quality Enhancement Retreat were asked to complete the I.E. Employee Survey. The following responses were received:

Table 2
Responses from I.E. Employee Survey

Full-time Faculty	107 of 117	91%
Part-time Faculty	83 of 450	18%
	190 of 567	34%
Full-time Staff	93 of 175	53%
Part-time Staff	14 of 73	19%
	107 of 248	43%

Similar to the student surveys, employee survey responses provided a positive assessment of A-B Tech's people as well as the learning and working environment. A-B Tech Invitational Education Employee Surveys also showed the following areas of concern.

Table 3
Invitational Education Employee Survey Concerns

Employee Survey Results	Faculty Response Strongly or tended to disagree	Staff Response Strongly or tended to disagree
2. "Adjunct/part-time instructors receive needed information, training, and resources."	52%	40%
5b. "Advisors rfeceive sufficient training for providing academic guidance to students."	27%	22%
33. "I receive timely notification of needed information."	31%	26%
42b. "I can find what I need on the A-B Tech intranet."	6%	6%
43b. "I can find what I need on the A-B Tech website."	8%	5%

46. "Advisees are seen in a reasonable amount of time."	1% (compared to 18% of students)	15%
47. "Advisors provide effective advising/guidance on curriculum course selections, program requirements, etc."	18%	12%
48. "adequate provisions are made for students whose advisors are 9-month."	25%	20%
49. "The registration process operates smoothly for curriculum students."	32%	28%

A-B Tech Invitational Education
Continuing Education Student Survey

When writing the invitational education student survey, the QET originally surmised that one survey would work for all AB-Tech students. It soon reconsidered, however, because Continuing Education has a diverse student population and is fundamentally different from the curriculum programs. The QET subsequently wrote a second survey specifically for Continuing Education students to ensure that the questions asked were both meaningful and applicable. Forty-seven questions relating to A-B Tech's People, Places, Programs, Policies and Processes were included, along with ample space for comments. At the end of the survey, students were asked, "Out of the questions asked, which ONE do you consider most important to your success as a student at A-B Tech?" and "What have we forgotten to ask that you really want us to know?" This survey was distributed throughout April and May of 2003. Of the 1,000 surveys distributed, 342 responded for a return rate of 34%.

Continuing Education student responses, like those for curriculum students, were overwhelmingly positive in support of A-B Tech's staff, faculty and learning environment. I.E. Continuing Education Student Survey results also showed the following areas of concern.

Table 3
Continuing Education Student Survey

Continuing Education Student Survey Results	Does Not or Somewhat Meets
1. "When I ask for information or assistance on campus, college employees are able to provide it for me."	7%
2. "When I leave messages through the college voice mail system, I receive a prompt and clear response to my message."	22%
7. "I know the name of my program's coordinator."	30% No
8. "Campus offices seem to have enough staff to handle questions and problems."	14%
10. "The college switchboard is able to transfer my call to the correct office when I need information."	18%
19. "When registering for classes, I know where to go and whom to see."	19%
29a. "I received a course outline (syllabus) on the first day of class."	30% No
30b. "I can find what I need on the A-B Tech website."	5%
38. "The registration process operates smoothly."	10%
43. "I am able to contact my instructors outside of class time."	25%

The invitational student surveys from curriculum and continuing education students not only supported the 5-P feedback received earlier from A-B Tech employees, but also clearly showed the impact of the 5-"P's" on the students' perceptions and experiences at A-B Tech.

For its final Quality Enhancement retreat, the QET retreat, the QET planned and offered five targeted "invitational" training sessions for the following groups:

Invitational Leadership
Target audience: *Supervisory/Professional Staff*

Invitational Advisement
Target audience: *Full-time Curriculum and Continuing Education Instructors*

Becoming Professionally and Personally Inviting
Target audience: *Office Professionals*

Invitational Teaching: Techniques from the NC Great Teachers Retreat
Target audience: *Continuing Education and Curriculum Part-Time Instructors*

Invitational Places
Target audience: *Plant Operations Personnel*

Defining the QEP through Invitational Education Activities

Following three College-wide QEP Retreats, the writing, distribution, and analysis of invitational education surveys of employees, curriculum and continuing education students (along with review and analysis of comprehensive, existing student survey data on student satisfaction, goal completion, retention, etc.), regularly scheduled QET meetings, and a number of visits to student, staff and faculty groups across the College, the QEP issue was further refined within "Developing Strategies for Student Success through Invitational Education" to the topic of "Educational and Career Advisement."

"Educational and Career Advisement" is the college-wide activity of communicating information to prospective and current students. It is not limited to one-on-one meetings to discuss schedule planning or career goals (although these activities are included in the focus.) Every A-B Tech employee advises students, whether formally or informally, every day. By intentionally improving the information communicated to students and each other as well as the process by which it is communicated, A-B Tech is becoming become more invitational and will thereby increase opportunities for student success. One measure of that success will be retention, along with increased student satisfaction (both of these items are regularly measured by A-B Tech.)

So...How Invitational are We?

The single, most important change at A-B Tech since beginning the invitational education journey is "intentionality." While many aspects of our College were already "unintentionally inviting," we now actively seek ways to invite our students and each other to be successful. During the on-site visit, one A-B Tech employee described this process as "evolving and involving."

One step towards achieving that goal is the adoption of a Vision Statement as part of our Strategic Plan: "*A-B Tech's vision is to develop strategies for student success through Invitational Education.*" This statement ensures that all future strategic planning that occurs at A-B Tech will be viewed through the through the lens of "invitational education." In addition, an "invitational protocol" (a series of questions to ask yourself during any decision-making process, such as "Have all parties involved been included in the discussion before a decision is made?") is being developed to assist in ensuring the "Invitability" of decisions and the communication of those decisions regarding A-B Tech's 5 "P's." Additionally, to help community colleges learn about invitational education from each other, in February, 2003, the International Alliance for Invitational Education named Deborah Lonon, QE Team Leader for A-B Tech, the IAIE Community College "Connector." In this role, Deborah and A-B Tech will serve as a resource for any community college in North America requesting information about invitational education. As a result of serving as "Connector," A-B Tech has shared in the research, for example, of Highland Community College, Highland, Kansas, where the Vice President for Student Services is developing a study on the relationship. Lastly, the former QE Team Leader has just been named the new "Invitational Education Coordinator/Instructor" to help ensure that A-B Tech becomes the "beacon" institution cited by the on-site visiting SACS team. What follows is a partial list of "Inviting" accomplishments that have occurred as the QEP process progressed.

Inviting Accomplishments:
A-B Tech's People, Places, Programs,
Policies, and Processes
(a partial listing!)

1. The Foundation Scholarship selection process has been reviewed and revised to ensure the successful continuity of students achieving their academic and career goals. *People, Programs, Processes.*

2. To assist in improving the cleanliness and maintenance of A-B Tech's buildings, automated work orders for plant operations have been implemented. *People, Places, Programs, Processes.*

3. Online registration for the Ed2Go classes has begun in the Continuing Education Division [Ed2Go classes are instructor-facilitated, 6-week, online courses in the areas of web graphics and design, web programming, the internet, desktop publishing, etc.] *People, Programs, Processes.*

4. Changes in the format and content of the College Catalog were designed to assist students and their advisors with course requirements and selection. *People, Programs, Processes.*

5. Changes in the associate degree advising check-off sheets were designed to assist Arts and Sciences Division students and their advisors with course requirements and selection. *People, Programs, Processes.*

6. The A-B Tech Café opened under new management with an updated menu and extended hours. *People, Places.*

7. The College designated outdoor smoking and non-smoking areas across its campuses. *People, Places, Policies.*

8. The Engineering and Applied Technology Division designed and staffed an advising program housed in the Student Services area during Fall 2003 registration. *People, Places, Programs, Processes.*

9. An intramurals program for staff and students was begun in January 2003. *People, Places, Programs.*

10. A-B Tech employees were asked to contribute a special talent as a prize for the 2002 Holiday dinner—a way to share our gifts within the A-B Tech community. *People, Processes.*

11. E-mail accounts were set up for all curriculum adjunct faculty and their names were included in the employee directory on the A-B Tech website in November, 2002. *People, Processes.*

12. *TechTalk* (A-B Tech's newsletter) has been utilized as a communications tool to ensure that A-B Tech employees are kept informed and invested in the QEP process. *People, Processes.*

13. "Invitational" workshops and presentations have been added to the Organization Development calendar. *People, Places, Programs, Processes.*

14. Student Services advisors may now register students at their own desks. *People, Places, Programs, Processes.*

15. An expanded departmental extension list will be added to A-B Tech's directory in the next BellSouth white pages. *People, Places.*

16. All employees have been invited to submit their ideas for naming streets at the Victoria Road campus of A-B Tech. *People, Places, Processes.*

17. Places for students to gather and study have been included in the new Balsam Building. *People, Places.*

18. Letters inviting students to participate in graduation have been reviewed for their "invitability." *People, Processes.*

19. New telephone emergency stickers were placed on every telephone, and emergency phones have been placed in building hallways. *People, Places, Programs, Processes.*

20. "Invitability" has become an attribute when interviewing candidates for new positions at A-B Tech. *People, Places, Processes.*

21. After hearing employee concern over the removal of trees, the architects received permission from the city to reduce the num-

ber of parking spaces in front of a new A-B Tech building, thus preserving the green space. *People, Places, Processes.*
22. The new College Transfer Advising Center is under construction and will open July 1, 2004. *People, Places, Programs, Policies, Processes.*
23. "Invitational" has been incorporated into the College's lexicon. *People, Places, Programs, Policies, Processes.*

Summary

From the beginning of the planning process, A-B Tech's Quality Enhancement Plan has been viewed as more than a requirement for reaffirmation of re-accreditation; it has provided an opportunity to create a significant, long-lasting, positive change that will have far-reaching effects for all of A-B Tech's students and employees. The use of invitational education has been an integral part of this process, one that has forever changed the way A-B Tech views and evaluates its success. While the QEP focus changed and narrowed over time, the original Quality Enhancement Team recommendation remains: that A-B Tech view the entire college as a "learning environment" through the lens of "invitational education" in order to assess how effectively A-B Tech assists students in meeting their goals.

References

Novak, J. M. & Purkey, W. W. *Invitational education fastback* (2001). *#488.* Bloomington, IN : Phi Delta Kappa Educational Foundation.

Purkey, W. W. & Novak, J.M. (1993). The invitational helix: A systemic guide for individual and organizational development. *Journal of Invitational Theory and Practice, 2*(2), 59-67.

Purkey, W.W. & Siegel, B. L. (2003) *Becoming an invitational leader: A new approach to professional and personal success.* Atlanta, GA: Humanics Trade Group.

Chapter 15

Sustaining
Inviting Schools

John M. Novak and Ann-Marie DiBiase

Creating inviting schools is about putting into practice imaginative acts of hope. The thirteen stories in this book energetically show how teachers, principals, superintendents, staff, parents, students, and university professors have worked to study, implement, evaluate, and savor inviting practices and possibilities. This certainly can be of value to educators who wish to begin the process of making their schools more vibrant and welcoming places. Beginnings, however, although they are necessary, should not be the end. Education is filled with strong starters, and exciting commencements. Energetic episodes of emotional engagement have their place, but some important follow-up questions need to be asked: "Are these practices sustainable?" "How long can people stay intentionally inviting?" "What happens when the initiators of these inviting changes leave?"

Education is filled with "Fads of the Month." High-minded, well-meaning people start impressive projects, and then they leave. What makes each of the stories in this book more powerful is that each points to the possibility of creating a deep and abiding culture of inviting. In such a culture, operating from an inviting stance becomes "the way things are done here." The assumptions, foundations, and strategies of the inviting perspective are internalized and transformed. Each of the stories here, points to an individual success and to the possibility of sustaining inviting schools.

For invitational education to be effective over time it has to touch the hearts, heads, and hands of all involved in the educative process. Invitational leaders are involved in the process of summoning, savoring, and sustaining imaginative acts of hope. Hope is about the heart. Invitational hope is about the persistence, resourcefulness, and courage needed to be involved for the long run. Each of the stories in this book showed these qualities either explicitly or implicitly, from starting an "inviting family school" near a military base to developing a Quality Enhancement Plan as a basis for study and growth for a community college.

The "head" of Invitational Education is the democratic, perceptual, self-concept theory of practice. Each of the stories showed the importance of having participants develop a deep understanding of the meaning of these concepts and how they might be creatively applied and extended, from working with staff in developing a mission statement in a kindergarten school to making connections with the wellness movement in South Africa. The "hand" of invitational education is its commitment to action. This handiwork is seen in the vibrant and ongoing work of Creative Primary School and Homantin Government Secondary School in Hong Kong. The inviting school movement started in Hong Kong is growing exponentially. With this connection to the heart, head, and hand working together, we can think more systematically about the process of sustaining invitational leadership.

Hargreaves (2005) has emphasized the importance of sustainable leadership, leadership that runs deep, stays around, and makes a difference for the long run. According to Hargreaves, sustainable leadership involves the following ten principles: (1) substance; (2) enduring; (3) diffusive; (4) socially just; (5) resourceful; (6) promotesdiversity and builds capacity; (7) activistic; (8) vigilant;

(9) respects the past; and (10) patient. These leadership principles can be looked at in terms of their applicability for creating *and* sustaining inviting schools.

Sustainable Leadership Principal One: Substance

For inviting schools to be sustained, people working in them need knowledge that has an edge, knowledge that runs deep and makes a real difference in how people perceive themselves and their life possibilities. This need for depth is two-fold for invitational leaders. First, there is a need for an in-depth understanding of the principles and ethical commitments of the inviting perspective. Without this in-depth understanding, inviting practices are not anchored to anything intellectually solid and will be blown away when the next educational storm occurs. Sue Bowen (Chapter 5), in her work as a curriculum superintendent, and Kate Asbill (Chapter 2) and Clio Chan (Chapter 10), as principals, showed the importance of emphasizing a solid foundation to work from while they were also developing concrete practices. Conversely, Nicky Alymer, Di Dawes, and Martyn van der Merwe (Chapter 13) note how it is difficult to get past the unintentionally inviting level if you only have a surface understanding of key ideas. Nice people doing nice things is nice, but the inviting perspective needs to go beyond niceness to sustain inviting schools in not-so-nice times.

On a second but related front, if inviting schools are going to last they need to teach subjects that matter to people who matter even more. Without an in-depth understanding of what is being taught and learned, and why and how it is being taught and learned, inviting schools are mere shells that have a nice appearance but lack sustenance. Sustenance, by definition, sustains. That which lacks sustenance withers. Withering heights of enthusiasm can come crashing down on disenchanted doers of good. This is why DiPetta, Novak, and Marini (Chapter 8) emphasize having prudent understanding of on-line education and a willingness to explore some of its myths. Mythbusting, done in a caring and conscientious way, helps people develop a healthy and lasting enthusiasm.

Sustainable Leadership Principal Two: Enduring

Sustainability, as Hargreaves (2005) points out, "preserves and advances the most valuable aspects of life over time" (p. 177). In education, people come and go, and with departure often are gone the benefits of their initiatives and their successes. If inviting schools are to become more like beacons that attract the growing attention of more and more people, then they need to make sure that they are not like ephemeral fireflies dependent on charismatic leaders and temporarily enthusiastic devotees. For preservation and success to last, there is a need to be intentional about what is carried forward. There is a need to have a plan for continuity. As Priscilla Lee and Wendy Ho (Chapter 11) show, Homantin Government Secondary School in Hong Kong had already won an inviting school award under Lillian Chan, the former principal. Building on what she had done, they were able to preserve and advance the invitational quality of the school. This did not happen by accident. Thoughtful planning about what happens after the initiators are gone is key to inviting sustainable leadership. With this in mind, the success in Garfield Heights that Judy Lehr and Ronald Victor (Chapter 6) write about also needs to be seen in terms of what has happened after Dr. Victor left.

Sustainable Leadership Principal Three: Diffusive

Sustaining inviting schools will not work if leadership is concentrated in the hands of a select few and others are expected merely follow their mandates. This top-down "doing-to" process is antithetical to the spirit of invitational education. Invitational leadership needs to be distributed among more and more people if the "doing-with" feeling of invitational education is to be sus-

252

tained. In fact, this process of distributing leadership in inviting ways is the means and ends of the inviting process. As John Dewey (1966/1916) pointed out, people exist in and through the process of communication. In the process of communication, Dewey noted, we hold things in common and become a community. This community-building process is vital for sustaining inviting schools. The work at Calcium Primary School reported by Wendy Rocca, Harvey Smith, and Lana Taylor (Chapter 3) shows the vibrancy that distributed leadership can take. The principal, teachers, staff, parents, students, and community members all take active leadership roles in spreading the word. The work at Calcium Primary School has been a shot heard around the world. Likewise, if the spirit and intentions of an inviting school are to be spread to parents in inviting ways, then educators need to make sure that they do not shoot themselves in the foot. Inviting parent participation, as Alice Schutz, Mary Louise Vanderlee and Rahul Kumar (Chapter 9) point out needs to follow well-established procedures for deliberation or people will feel that they have been "done-to" or "done-in" rather than "done-with."

Sustainable Leadership Principal Four: Socially Just

The theory and practice of invitational education is a part of a larger project of social justice that strives to call forth the development of all human beings. The democratic ethos, the first foundation of invitational education, is an ethical and political commitment to the ideal that all people matter and have a right to participate meaningfully in the rules that regulate their lives. This emphasis on social justice in the larger world is a commitment to create the social conditions that reduce ignorance, cruelty, and poverty. The emphasis on caring schools in South Africa that development wellness, as reported by Linda Theron and Martyn van der Merwe (Chapter 13), takes seriously the idea to address previous injustices.

There is also a need to address social justice in the internal world of a school system. Invitational schools need to play fair within the school system and make sure that they do not get more than their share of human and physical resources. Unfair treatment builds up resentment from others within the system that can lead to intentional and unintentional sabotage of inviting efforts. The "doing-with" spirit of inviting schools has to apply to their relationship with other schools in the system. The sense that "we are all in it together" needs to be made manifest in the everyday discussions and negotiations for resources. Building a cadre of resentment from other schools can drain the life out of an inviting school. The system-wide approach of Ronald Victor (Chapter 6) is an important part of creating the conditions that invite sustainability.

Sustainable Leadership Principal Five: Resourceful

One way to cut down on resentment from other schools over the fight for limited resources is to develop alternative sources for material and human resources. Key to the success at Calcium Primary School is its ability to use creative ways to invite people to come to the school and use their skills and fundraising abilities to make good things happen. Car washes and garage sales were just a few of the activities that administration, teachers, and staff used to raise money to take a bus trip to Virginia Beach to collectively receive their Inviting School Award. The administration and staff at Calcuim Primary School thoughtful behaviour, serve as an impetus for positive and inviting interaction. That is, they find ingenious ways to develop resources. To do so in ways that are renewing rather than draining is a vital part of sustaining inviting schools. The work at St. John Neumann by Barbara Cole (Chapter 4) shows persistent and resourceful ways to keep parents informed, involved, and invited. Many potential resources are there just waiting to be involved.

Sustainable Leadership Principal Six: Promotes Diversity and Builds Capacity

Invitational education is built on an evolving theory of ethical practice. It is not some monolithic structure imposed on all settings. Taking seriously the idea that human uniqueness is not to be negated, inviting institutions build on what makes them special. This is beautifully illustrated by Deborah Lonon (Chapter 14) in the work done at Ashville-Buncombe Technical Community College. Rather than rely on a standard evaluation tool to assess the work of their institution, the administrators, instructors, and staff developed a plan that emphasized their uniqueness and special mission. In the process of doing this, individuals at Ashville-Buncombe Technical Community College built the diverse leadership capacity of all involved. They even provided hard data to show the positive results of what they have done. Part of sustaining inviting institutions is to realize the potential for creative flexibility in what are often seen as rigid bureaucratic structures. There are cracks in the bureaucratic egg and some creative educational omelets are waiting to be called forth. Negotiating these bureaucratic cracks is a way to bring new vitality to a constricting system. On a more individual level, Tommie Radd (Chapter 7) show how the uniqueness of students can be honored by using classroom "life labs" that build on the perceptual and self-concept foundations of invitational education. Diversity and capacity develops when students can see themselves as valuable, able, and responsible participants in meaningful activities. Teachers and staff develop and extend these ideas as they model them in their own behaviour.

Sustainable Leadership Principal Seven:
Activistic

Invitational education emphasizes the importance of intentional behavior. Doing things on purpose, for purposesm one can defend is key to creating inviting schools. This proactive spirit needs to be retained if inviting schools are to be sustained. The work of Creative Primary School (Chapter 10) is an excellent example of not "rusting on your laurels." Setting up communication networks with Sue Bowen's (Chapter 5) contact, Superintendent Dallas Blankenship in Kentucky, and Peter Wong in Hong Kong, there have been ongoing teacher and principal exchanges between Hong Kong and

Scott County, Kentucky, that have brought even more life to already creative systems. Sustainability thrives through alliances and personal contact with kindred spirits. These professional alliances and personal contacts are especially important when the outside environment is less that inviting. Being the "Lone Inviter," although possible, it difficult to sustain. Speaking out on educational issues is easier when you know that there are people on your side.

Sustainable Leadership Principal Eight:
Vigilant

John Dewey (1966/1916) postulated that growth was the end of education. By that he meant that learning to appreciate, understand, and improve more of your individual and collective experiences is the means and purpose of education. In the process of growing, we learn to appreciate the present and grow even more. Building on the idea that that which stifles growth is anti-educative, inviting schools need to be seen in terms of how they are savoring what they have accomplished and how they are getting better as a result meaningful work. Accomplishments need to be celebrated in the present and means to further growth. That is what makes the success of Ashville-Buncombe Technical Community College so refreshing. They have reaffirmed themselves through the re-accreditation process. They have shown how "Superior rated" learning institution is becoming even better. There is a palpable sense of growth on the campus and in the community. By looking for tangible measures of inviting and disinviting practices, they are ahead of the process.

Sustainable Leadership Principal Nine:
Respects the Past

Although the rhetoric of the glass half empty has a certain appeal, people tend to be suspicious of those who only see them in terms of what they might be. Visionaries who only look to the future overlook an appreciation of the present, and negate the achievements of the past. That sends very disinviting messages to those who happen to have pasts and inhabit the present. To live only for the future is to always want to be someplace other than where you are. It is to be disengaged from the present. People have difficulty sustaining on-going relationships with such disengaging visionaries. The same is true for trying to sustain inviting schools. As Hargreaves (2005) points out, "sustainable leadership respects and builds on the past in its quest to build a better future" (p.185). Looking at the past as a source of wisdom and learning, Homontin Government Secondary Schools (Chapter 11) honors the work of previous educators and community members. Such an appreciation comes back to the school in terms of the community's support for their students and their activities. There is much to be learned from around the world in terms of developing continuity with the past. The North American tendency to emphasize "the latest, the greatest" can lead to becoming great re-inventors of that which has been around for a long time.

Sustainable Leadership Principal Ten:
Patient

Invitational schools are filled with energy. There seems to be always something new happening, with the promise of even more to come in the not-too-distant future. That being said, inviting schools were not developed overnight and much of the good that will come from them has not even been imagined. Much of the work at Calcium Primary School (Chapter 3) with separated military families will not be seen for many years. The promise of the quick result necessary for political expediency needs to be put in perspective if inviting schools are going be sustained. Some of the essential work of creating inviting schools is about planting seeds that may or may not come to fruition in expected ways. Kate Asbill's (Chapter 2) work on modeling the inviting approach and Sue Bowen's (Chapter 5) conversational style both take time, patience, and respect for their potential participant's necessity to process things in their own way. The patience in the inviting process is a faith in the ability and

257

desire of people of good will to come together and make even better things happen. That patience, when matched with a pragmatic hope based on persistence, resourcefulness, and courage works to sustain inviting schools.

Conclusion

Each of the stories in this book provided some insight on aspects of the principles for sustaining inviting schools. However, no one story covered all ten principles. Focusing on deep learning that lasts and can spread to many people in the school and beyond is certainly necessary, but it is not sufficient. Likewise, emphasizing an active social justice program that is resourceful and promotes diversity as it builds capacity is certainly industrious, but it too is no guarantee of sustainability. Similarly, stressing a patient vigilance that respects the past and sets a prudent course provides possibilities but gives no final assurances. It is this artful blending of necessity, industry, and prudence in the face of promise and uncertainty that marks the context for creating and sustaining inviting schools. The job of invitational leaders is to create and sustain the conditions necessary for imaginative acts of hope to come forth, develop, and flourish (Novak, 2002). This is challenging work in which there are no final guarantees, but there is the experience and promise of even deeper and more lasting connections to people, ideas, and adventures. This is being done all the time in all parts of the world. It is the job of people of good will to make sure it keeps on happening.

References

Dewey, J. (1966/1916). *Democracy and education: An introduction to the philosophy of education.* New York: The Free Press. (First published in 1916).

Hargreaves, A. (2005). Sustainable leadership. In B. Davies (Ed.) *The essentials of school leadership* (pp. 173-189). London, UK: Paul Chapman.

Novak, J. (2002). *Inviting educational leadership: Fulfilling potential and applying an ethical perspective to the educational process.* London, UK: Pearson.

Contributing
Authors

Nicky Aylmer (Nicolette Ann) is a senior primary school teacher with 30 years of experience. Nicky lives in Johannesburg, South Africa, with her husband and three adult children. In 2001, she attended Rand Afrikaans University to complete her honours degree in Special Needs Education, choosing Invitational Education as one of her modules. Currently, she is completing her Masters in Learner Support. She is the owner of a tutoring, home schooling/assisted learning facility that works with children with special needs.

Kate Asbill was the principal of two schools that received the Inviting School Award and (working as an Invitational Education consultant) she has assisted six other schools in earning that distinction.

Sue Bowen served as a school administrator in West Virginia and Kentucky for 28 years. She served as Executive Director of the International Alliance for Invitational Education in 2002-2003.

Chan So Ming (Clio), M.Ed. is the Principal of Creative Primary School, Hong Kong. She is a founding member and Chairlady of the International Alliance for Invitational Education (Hong Kong).

Barbara Cole is in her fifteenth years as a principal and in her twenty-third year in education. Her experience ranges from second grade through college. Coming from the Midwest, Barbara finds herself in Columbia, South Carolina, enjoying every day at the best school in the world, thanks to the caring parents, loving children, and dedicated professional faculty and staff. She and her husband, Nick, a librarian, have two children: Jennifer, who is a teacher in Covington, Georgia, and a son, Erik, who is in the Army.

Ann-Marie DiBiase is Assistant Professor of Educational Psychology in the Department of Graduate and Undergraduate Studies of the Faculty of Education at Brock University. Dr. DiBiase's research has concerned psychopathological behaviour and emotional and behavioural disorders of children and youth, and prevention/ intervention programs for children at risk for antisocial behaviour (anger management, social skills development, and moral reasoning). She has recently published a book that addresses psychoeducational prevention/intervention entitled *EQUIP for Educators: Teaching Youth (Grades 5-8) to Think and Act Responsibly* (DiBiase, Gibbs, & Potter, 2005).

Tony DiPetta is a teacher-educator with over 20 years experience working across the education sector. He has been a training and adult education consultant for business, industry, and the Canadian military, as well as having taught in secondary schools, community colleges, and faculties of education in Ontario and New Brunswick. Dr. Di Petta has worked as the co-ordinator of training for the Education Network of Ontario and as an on-line moderator for the NODE network for distance education. Currently he is an Associate Professor of Education at Brock University where he teaches in the technological education program and the pre-service teacher program. His research interests include technology in education, the social, cognitive, and cultural impact of virtual environments, and invitational approaches to humanizing technology design and use.

Wendy Ho obtained her degree in English Literature from the Chinese University of Hong Kong and started her teaching career in the late 1970s. She has also served as a teacher counselor and obtained two Master's degrees, one in Guidance and Counseling and another in Translation. In addition to being involved in the development of inviting schools in Hong King, she has just been made principal or Hotung Secondary School.

Rahul Kumar is the Manager of Computer Services and a Ph.D. candidate (Policy and Leadership) in the Faculty of Education at Brock University. His research interests are ethics in leadership, role of technology in education, and administrative policy development.

Priscilla Lee graduated in 1975 with a B.Sc. Degree in Physics and Math. Priscilla taught grade 7 to grade 13 for 19 years before working as an Assistant Principal for five years. She also worked in the Advisory Inspectorate as Senior Inspector to inspect schools and assist in the development of School Performance Indicators in the Education Department for one year. Mrs. Lee is currently the Principal of Homantin Government Secondary School, Hong Kong.

Judy Brown Lehr is currently an Associate Professor at The Citadel in Charleston, South Carolina. Judy is co-author of the popular book published by the National Education Association, *The At-Risk, Low-Achieving Student in the Classroom*. She has served as a consultant and keynote speaker on Invitational Education for school districts throughout the United States, Europe, and Canada.

Deborah Lonon is the new Invitational Education Coordinator/ Instructor at Asheville-Buncombe Technical Community College in Asheville, North Carolina. In addition to promoting the tenets of Invitational Education, she teaches English and Speech and serves as Director and Founder of the A-B Tech Readers Theatre Troupe.

Zopito Marini is a developmental and educational psychologist, currently a Full Professor in the Department of Child and Youth Studies at Brock University. Dr. Marini did his graduate work at the Ontario Institute for Studies in Education at the University of Toronto with Robbie Case, and has been at Brock since 1985, where he was the founding Chair of the Department. Dr. Marini does research, and writes and lectures on issues related to school conflicts and their effect on children's learning. A number of projects are currently underway in his lab dedicated to making schools more inviting, including examining the role of technology as well as peers (i.e., bullying and victimization) on the learning process.

John M. Novak is Professor of Education at Brock University and President of the Society of Professors of Education. At Brock University he has been Chair of the Department of Graduate Studies in Education, President of the Brock University Faculty Board, and a member of the Board of Trustees. An active speaker and writer, he has given invited talks on six continents and has spoken north of the Arctic Circle and in the south of New Zealand. Recent books and monographs he authored or co-authored are *Inviting Educational Leadership, Inviting On-Line Education, Invitational Education, Inviting School Success,* and *Democratic Teacher Education.*

Tommie R. Radd is an educational expert, redefining the way schools worldwide develop guidance and counseling programs, giving students greater odds of achieving life success. For more than three decades as an educational and counseling strategist Dr. Radd has been finding solutions to important issues confronting students, teachers, school counselors, and administrators, using a team-integrated approach. Dr. Radd lectures and consults for school districts and education departments around the world, designing innovative programs to best meet their needs. A Professor of Counselor Education at the University of Nebraska at Omaha, Dr. Radd holds a doctorate in elementary education curriculum and instruction from the University of Akron. She is a licensed professional counselor holding National Board Certifications and numerous counseling, teaching, and administrative certifications.

Wendy Rocca, M.Ed. has recently received a Master of Education and is in the process of completing the Pre-Service Program at Brock University. Additionally, she teaches courses at the local college and is a teaching assistant in the Education Department at Brock University.

Harvey Smith did his undergraduate work at the State University of New York at Oswego, followed by graduate work at Indiana State University and Syracuse University, and is presently a Professor Emeritus and Campus Minister at the State University of New York at Potsdam. Dr. Smith has had a wide range of experience in teacher education, including both elementary and secondary school teaching, and administrative experience as a public school principal and a college dean. He has presented workshops and keynote addresses on the topics of Leadership, Invitational Education, and Developing A Positive Self-Concept throughout the United States, Canada, South Africa, and Hong Kong. His very popular graduate course entitled, "Developing A Positive Self-Concept," has been in demand for over 25 years.

Alice Schutz is an Assistant Professor in the Graduate Department at Brock University's Faculty of Education. She teaches courses in Curriculum, Reflective Practice, and Gender Issues. Her main interests are creativity, gifted education, role modeling and mentoring, and issues related to student learning and teacher development.

Lana Taylor holds Colorado State Administrative Certification, New York State Administrative Certification (SDA) 1991, and is the Principal of the Calcium Primary School. Lana has 35 years of experience as a life-long educator and is an accomplished teacher and administrator. She has served as an educational consultant for the International Alliance for Invitational Education in Washington, D.C., and Hong Kong, presenting several workshops throughout the U.S., Canada, and Hong Kong. Lana has provided instructional workshops on Inviting Schools and Peace Education for Jefferson-Lewis BOCES staff development courses. She was selected by the Fort Drum Masonic Lodge to receive an award for outstanding community service. As principal of Calcium Primary, she received the "Inviting School" award given by the International Alliance for Invitational Education. Calcium Primary School has also been honored as a successful inviting school in the #488 Fastback published by the Phi Delta Kappa Educational Foundation.

Linda Theron is a practising educational psychologist and a senior lecturer in Educational Psychology at the North-West University of South Africa. She obtained her doctoral degree in Educational Psychology in 2000 and joined the University in the same year. She lectures post-graduate students and is primarily involved in research focusing on resilience and on the impact of the HIV and AIDS pandemic on affected educators in South Africa. Currently, Linda holds a National Research Foundation grant to research this impact. She has published several related articles and delivered papers at national and international conferences. Five doctoral and four master's students have completed related theses under her guidance.

Martyn van der Merwe is a Senior Lecturer at the Johannesburg University in South Africa. His teaching and research focusses on Invitational Education as an approach to facilitate inclusion in schools and to combat bullying in schools.

Mary-Louise Vanderlee, Ed. is an Assistant Professor in the Faculty of Education at Brock University and specializes in early childhood education and parent involvement in children's schooling. Additionally, she has spent over 10 years actively participating in and researching parent and school councils.

Ronald L. Victor retired from the Garfield Heights City Schools in July of 2004 after serving as superintendent of schools for 12 and a half years and has completed his doctoral degree from The University of Akron. His more than 34 years of practical experience includes work as a teacher, guidance counselor, assistant principal, business manager, superintendent of schools, and, most recently, President of Leadership Ideas LLC.